LEATHER BRAIDING

by Bruce Grant

Illustrated by Larry Spinelli

CORNELL MARITIME PRESS, INC.

CENTREVILLE   MARYLAND

ISBN 10: 0-87033-039-X
ISBN 13: 978-0-87033-039-1

Library of Congress Catalog Card Number: 60-7746

Manufactured in the United States of America
First edition, 1950. 2005 reprint

LEATHER BRAIDING

Braided bridle shown on the famous stallion "Fact," which was presented to Averell Harriman by Premier Stalin of Russia. Bridle, made by author, contains more than 500 feet of leather thong.

To My MOTHER Who Was Thoughtful
Enough To See That I Was Born
In Texas

Leather picture frame decorated with applique braid and round
buttons and held together by "S" type applique (Pl. 74).

ACKNOWLEDGMENTS

Besides the recognized authorities I have consulted in print on the subject of leather braiding and thong work, I would like to thank for encouragement, moral support and helpful suggestions, the following: George Biderman, New York City; Gail Borden, Chicago; Jim Breslin, La Junta, Colo.; C. Bruce Chapin, New York City; Professor J. Frank Dobie, of Texas; Robert M. Denhardt, editor, The Western Horseman; David Eisendrath, Brooklyn, N.Y.; Martin Gardner, New York City; E. Richmond Gray, Winnetka, Ill.; D. Carlos Rincon Gallardo, Mexico City; Harry D. Hamilton, Whittier, Calif.; Suzelle F. Howes, New York City; Morgan Heap, Sun Valley, Idaho; Wayne C. Leckey, Popular Mechanics; J. C. Larson, of the J. C. Larson Leather Co., Chicago; Senor Abraham Nettor y Alexna, Buenos Aires; J. L. Nelson, secretary, Tanners Council of America; Fred Picard, New York City; Elmer J. Rumpf, editor, Hide and Leather and Shoes Weekly; Dr. Adolph Schubert, of the B. F. Eisendrath Tanning Company, Racine, Wis.; Edward Larocque Tinker, New York City; Dr. Karl Vogel, New York City; James R. Ward, editor, Shop Notes and Crafts, Popular Mechanics; Harry Walton, Home and Workshop Editor, Popular Science; Lt. Col. D. Douglas Young, Abercrombie & Fitch, New York City.

B.G.

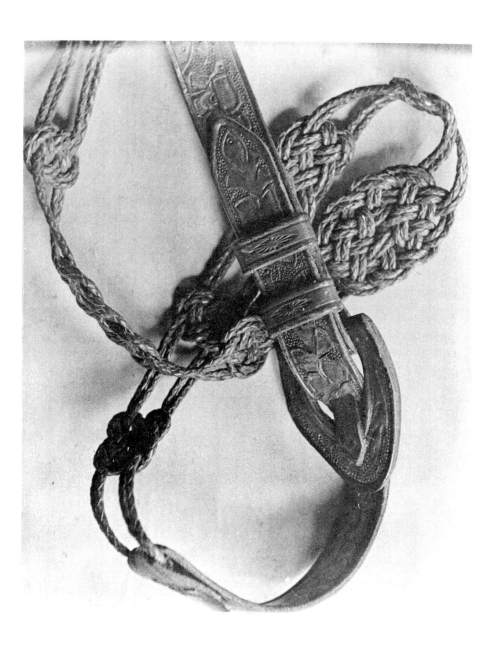

Belt made from a four thong round braid (without core, 50 feet after braided, Pl. 14) and then tied in Chinese knots.

CONTENTS

SQUARE BRAIDS

BUTTONS

EDGE LACING

BUCKLE COVERING

HANDLE COVERING

SPANISH KNOTS AND TURK'S HEADS

The Romance of
LEATHER BRAIDING

When man first realized what a useful and serviceable thing his own skin was he got busy trying to figure out how he could turn to practical account the skins and hides of other animals. This was the genesis of leather and the beginning of civilization.

With the skins and pelts prehistoric man tanned or cured he was able to clothe himself and thus hunt and forage during the winter months and travel and search for game in colder climates. He could make more comfortable homes in which to live, put together better tools with which to work, manufacture boats in which to cross streams, and assemble more efficient weapons for waging war.

Leather was an important factor during the remote Stone Age and while there is slight chance of archeologists ever discovering any of the actual leather apparel and craftsmanship of primitive man, the uses of leather have been revealed from sculptures and drawings found on walls of prehistoric caves. This crude art dates back from 20,000 years B.C. and indicates that man and his mate dressed in hides and skins.

However, pieces of leather articles, including light caps, aprons and undressed goat skins have been found in Egyptian tombs of 2,500 B.C.

Man's weapons metamorphosed from stone to bronze and from bronze to steel. Other things changed in his life and his ways of living, but not leather. He tanned the hides in much the same fashion as before and he utilized the leather in a similar way. Even in this day of the Atomic Age the preparation of leather has changed but little.

What is more interesting from our viewpoint is that man's ingenuity was challenged to find means of joining pieces of leather, fastening leather to other materials and shaping leather in forms to suit his needs. He used leather thongs for a wide variety of purposes. He sewed his garments together with them, he secured his war-heads to his weapons with them, he made ropes, handles and buttons, and he used leather thongs for hinges and leather for buckles and brads in place of the various metal fastenings common today.

Thus is leather associated with man in his transition from the brute into the thinking and reasoning individual, from the ignorant into the cultured, and from the cultured into the artistic. He used leather more and more and at one period the things he made represented the highest state of artistic development and his leather handcraft was a most beautiful and attractive art.

The actual tanning of leather has been traced to the Bronze Age, which is roughly estimated from 2,500 to 800 B.C. Prior to that it is believed that primitive man preserved his hides in a more or less pliable and imputrescible condition by treating the pelts with the grease and brains of the animal itself, much after the fashion in which American Indians make their buckskin. Or, as the Eskimos do today, early man might have used urine in tanning his leather.

It is certain that a chrome, formaldehyde or alum tannage was unknown.

However, during the Bronze Age the fleshy sides of the hides were rubbed with salt and alum, stored in cool places for a few days and then stretched and pulled. The fatty sides were scraped and limestone sand rubbed in. The skins were stretched and dried.

This method came down to the Romans who perfected it in producing their fine leather known as *aluta*. This soft leather was said to have even been used by the Roman ladies for fashioning their "beauty spots."

The Greeks, also, were adepts in the tanning and utilization of leather. The first Greek leather worker is cited as Tychios of Boetia, a native of Hyle. He is credited by Homer with having made the shield of Ajax, and Pliny termed him the inventor of tanning.

In those days leather and skins were used for beds, blankets, rugs, curtains, coverings for chairs and couches, and for shoes as well as for many other purposes. A deerskin bed was believed to protect the sleeper against snakes and priests slept on special skins when they wished to invoke oracles in their dreams.

The Bible contains frequent mention of leather. In Genesis iii 21 we find: "Unto Adam also and to his wife did the Lord God make coats of skins, and clothed them." It also tells that Moses dyed rams' skins.

In Butler's Lives of the Saints he writes of St. Crispin and St. Crispinian working with their hands at night making shoes. St. Crispin today is the patron saint of the shoemakers, and this honorable trade can boast such American examples as Noah Worcester, D.D., known as the Apostle of Peace; Roger Sherman, the patriot; Henry Wilson, the Natik Cobbler, and John Greenleaf Whittier, the Quaker Poet.

Hans Sachs, the shoemaker poet of Nuremberg, known as the Nightingale of the Reformation, in 1568 wrote a verse in which he told how he prepared his own leather:

> *"I dry the skins out in the air*
> *Removing first each clinging hair.*
> *Then in the Escher stream I dash them*
> *And thoroughly from dirt I wash them.*

ow-skin and calf in tan I keep,
Long months in bark-soaked water steep
Then with a brush of hair I scrape them
And on the selling counter drape them."

There are many wise and pithy sayings having to do with leather. One proverb has it, "Men cut large thongs from other men's leather." Unemotional men are said to have "thick hides," or they are "thick-skinned," while those with stubborn ideas are "hide-bound." We still use such expressions as "I'll tan your hide," "He's a skinflint," and "Give him a leather medal."

Carlyle in his *Sartor Resartus* comes to the conclusion that the old-world grazier became sick of lugging his slow ox about the country till he got it bartered for corn or oil, and would take a piece of leather and thereon stamp or scratch the mere figure of an ox, or *pecus.* He would put this in his pocket and call it *pecunia,* or money. Here is the derivation of our word *pecuniary,* and even today in modern slang we speak of a dollar bill as a "skin." We "skin" a man in a trade and when we do him out of something illegally it is by use of the "skin-game."

Ancient history is replete with references to leather and leather work. Unbelievable as it might seem there were even leather cannon! These guns, in calibers from 1-pounders to 4-pounders, consisting of a copper tube covered with several layers of mastic and wrapped with rope or twine on top of which was put a coat of plaster, were finally covered with leather. They were used as early as 1349 by the Venetians.

There were, of course, leather cups, leather bottles, leather chests and many other utility articles of leather. There is a complete literature on leather bookbinding and ancient leathercraft. Leather was in wide use—and even today there is hardly a person who does not have some form of leather about him—shoes, hatbands, pocketbooks, billfolds and such.

The most important of the historical notices on leather—from our viewpoint—has to do with the ancient Phoenicians. These people invaded North Africa probably in or around the year 1600 B.C. and transmitted their leathercraft to the Moors.

The Moors at the beginning of the Eighth Century crossed the Straits of Gibraltar and penetrated Spain. Here they inaugurated a brilliant civilization. In Cordova, the capital, the leather industry gave origin to several trades, one of which was harness-making. What leathers are more famous than Cordovan, Spanish and Morocco!

The *guadamacileros* of Spain could not be surpassed for their wonder creations of figured leather, for unlike the heavily lacquered and painted leathers of today these Spanish artists always subordinated their decorations to the leather itself. The leather never lost character. This art originated in the city of Ghadames in the Sahara, where the ghadamesian leather came from.

From the Ninth to the 18th centuries Europe had been reconquered and the Arabs expelled. But they left behind them not only their leather art, which included elaborate braiding and thong work, but their techniques for executing these things.

So in 1520 when Hernando Cortes introduced the first horses into America, he brought, too, men well versed in the understanding and teaching of leatherwork and the art of braiding.

It is not difficult from that point to trace the introduction of fancy braidwork into the United States. The Mexican *vaqueros* who rode the dusty trails of the plains and brought up their cattle from below the Rio Grande and those of the pre-gold rush cattle drives of California during the last century were expert *trenzadores,* or braiders. They were masters of leather braiding and leather decoration. Some were *charros* to whom the horse and his decoration or equipage was the primary object of life.

These Mexicans inspired our own cowboys to take pride in their gear and in those times a braided bridle with fancy woven knots scattered along the reins was a beautiful thing to behold. Not to speak of the hatbands, belts, pistol holsters, saddles, quirts and other gear and appurtenances.

The Spanish craft of leather braiding and decoration spread, too. It would be interesting to an anthropologist or archeologist to trace, for example, the Spanish woven knot, built upon the sailor's well-known turk's-head knot. I have seen woven finger rings of split bamboo made by the Igorotes of the Philippines which are exactly like those knots on Spanish and Arabian whip and knife handles.

The Argentine *gaucho* makes the same type of woven knot as does the native Indian of Mexico. The entire course of Spanish civilization could well be traced through this intricate and decorative knot.

The term "lost art" might be applied to leather braiding. However, it is a loose and generic term used in connection with most handcraft today. The greater part of our handcraft should be designated as a developed art. We continually see where improvements have been made in ancient worksmanship by the use of modern scientific methods and by machine operation and cultivated design.

Just as the development of the bow and arrow in archery makes these modern implements far superior to those of the ancients, especially the savages, so is textile weaving and many other arts and crafts as far advanced.

It might be better to say that leather braiding is an almost forgotten and highly neglected art. It is not necessary now to join things with leather thongs. Sewing with thread and fastening with metal brads are the methods used. The attractive and sometimes unique means of using leather buttons and other leather fastenings has been supplanted by all manner of metal devices.

In this book the broad term of "braiding" is used throughout much after the manner in which it is used by the Spanish *trenzador* and the craftsmen of Mexico and Latin America in general. Actually braiding means to weave together, to plait, and usually is associated with the so-called flat braid, or the three-thong "hair braid," or the simple braids used in making belts.

For our purpose it will mean the weaving of leather knots, the making of buttons, the working of edge lacing on leather articles, the covering of belt buckles, the appliquéd work on leather which is here introduced to the American public for the first time, and the beautiful one-thong weave which the Spanish *conquistadores* used on their sword belts, as well as many variations of the commonly known round and flat braids.

There still are a few old time braiders in the West and Southwest. Most of these guard their secrets well and like those who have gone before them, these secrets will be passed on to a very few, if any, and in many cases will die with the craftsmen. Through all the ages leathercraft has been an esoteric art, usually handed down from father to son.

Leather braidwork has many forms and many applications. You don't make things just to look at and admire, but to use. You combine beauty with utility. This work can be used in making handles for suitcases, brief cases and other leather articles. It adapts itself to use on and associated with plain or carved or tooled leather work, supplementing and complementing such examples of craftsmanship.

It can be used in covering the handles of canes, umbrellas and tools. It is, of course, employed in the making of quirts, riding crops, belts and wristwatch straps, dog collars and leashes, hackamores, bridles and reins, leather buttons, buckle coverings and for many, many other practical things.

The rewards of a small amount of work are ample and highly gratifying. There is another thing that should not be overlooked: the practicability of this handcraft for those persons who are convalescing or who are partially disabled or have some permanent injury which confine them to their beds or wheelchairs. The few tools necessary, the small amount of space in which the work can be done and the cleanliness with which it can be executed, make it uniquely adaptable in such cases. Its value in occupational and recreational therapy cannot be ignored.

While this book is primarily for those interested in leathercraft, the methods of braiding in nearly all cases are applicable to strands of many other materials—silk, cotton, plastic, rawhide, catgut or horsehair.

Especial care has been exercised in giving detailed step-by-step instruction methods, both in diagrams and text. It has been presumed that the reader knows nothing of braidwork and wants each move carefully explained.

In the years of my study of this subject—in Europe, South America and among Mexicans, Basque sheep herders, cowboys and others—I have picked up many things of value. I have worked out many types of braidwork, which have suggested themselves from the basic principles commonly in practice. Possibly they are not new but many are now shown in print for the first time.

As to turk's-heads and woven knots the methods employed in illustrating them and how to make them are at least an innovation. By the use of diagram patterns any type of turk's-head or woven knot, no matter how complicated, can be made by a method which is foolproof.

As a native of Texas, it is sincerely hoped these efforts will arouse interest in a craft which is identified with the tradition of our plainsmen and of our West and Southwest. Would you believe that there is no such thing as a museum collection in this country of cowboy handcraft—of braided bridles, hackamores, quirts *(cuartas)*, or *reatas,* nor even of stamped and carved leatherwork! It is a definite part of our folklore and has a positive archeological and anthropological value.

Fifty years from now museums will be digging around frantically in an endeavor to assemble a representative collection of the handcraft of the cowboy. But it will have vanished.

BRUCE GRANT.

Drum-head type woman's pocketbook showing carved work set off by 7-thong circular applique braid (similar to that of Pl. 77) and with Spanish edge braiding of three loops (Pl. 33). Braid work is in black and pocketbook natural calf.

PLATE 1

LEATHER-BRAIDING TOOLS—In leather braiding and thong work the best tool is the hand. Just as other tools must be sharpened and well cared for, so must this most valued tool; the sharpening in this instance is its development and training, which involves a certain mental process leading to the coordination of eye and hand.

The actual tools themselves are mere projections of the hands. To use tools properly one must become so familiar with them, with their feel, with their application and their purpose that it is possible to use them with the same dexterity as the hand. Most tools can do more harm than good in unpracticed hands.

Some people have a natural born deftness and knack for braiding and thong work; others acquire it only through careful and conscientious study and application—by hard and faithful practice. Yet, taken step by step, and each step carefully and accurately performed, it is, as is any handicraft, relatively simple.

A good knife is important. It may be a pocketknife or the type of knife known as the skiving knife (Fig. 1). Keep the knife sharp at all times.

Figs. 2 and 3 show thonging chisels for cutting slits in leather. A lacing needle (Fig. 5), purposely shown over-sized, is necessary for working with small thongs. The revolving punch with tubes (Fig. 4) which cuts holes of six different diameters, is an essential part of the equipment. A drive punch (Fig. 6), which may be had in different sizes, is also a necessary tool, in order to make holes several inches from the edge of the leather, which cannot be made with a revolving punch.

The fid, with a tapering metal part and blunt on the end, is a most valuable tool (Fig. 7). The space marker is a convenience, especially when lacing leather parts together, as it evenly marks the holes through which the thongs must pass (Fig. 8).

To cut belts or wide thongs from skins and hides, a draw gauge is used (Fig. 9). A mallet (Fig. 10) and dividers (Fig. 11) are also necessary.

For making Turk's-Heads or woven knots of leather a mandrel is needed. This can be made with six inches of common broomstick. Cement a collar of leather near one end, file the other down on four sides and number these surfaces from 1 to 4 in a clockwise direction (Fig. 12).

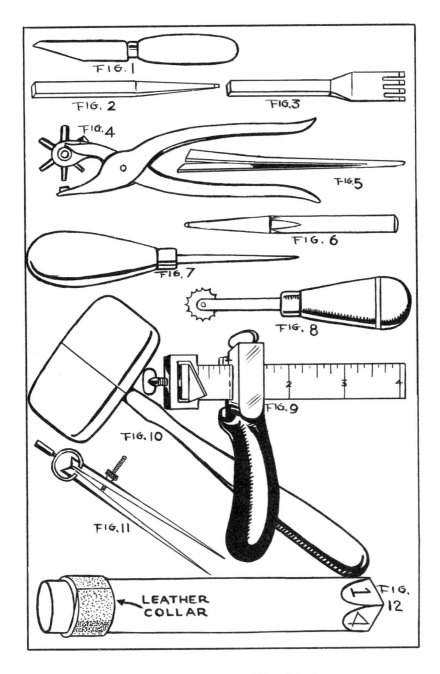

FIG. 1

FIG. 2

FIG. 3

FIG. 4

FIG. 5

FIG. 6

FIG. 7

FIG. 8

FIG. 9

FIG. 10

FIG. 11

LEATHER COLLAR

FIG. 12

PLATE 1—Leather Braiding Tools.

PLATE 2

THONG CUTTING—Some braiders prefer to cut their own thongs. These should be taken from that portion of the skin or hide that presents the least spongy appearance. Lay the leather on a hard cutting board and with a straight edge or ruler and a sharp knife cut the thongs, always cutting across the grain in the wood so the knife cannot follow this grain.

Scraps of leather may be cut into discs from four to eight inches in diameter. With a pair of shears, cut around the circumference the width of the thong desired (Fig. 1). After the thong is cut, its spiral shape can be straightened out by stretching it on the convex or inner side of the curve.

Some whipmakers cut their thongs freehand with a sharp knife, using the thumb as a gauge (Figs. 2 and 3). A more practical way is to use a thong cutter constructed as in Fig. 5. Other homemade thong cutters are shown in Figs. 6 and 7.

In cutting thongs it is important that the leather disc have a perfectly even circumference; also that the disc is laid out in the manner shown in Fig. 4, so that a *leader* is first cut. Make the circle segment for the leader by placing the point of the compass a fraction of an inch above the center of the first circle. Start the leader with a knife or shears.

In cutting a thong, either with a thong cutter or a draw gauge (Fig. 9), *pull only on the thong itself*.

The other illustrations show the uses of a few of the tools already mentioned. Dividers can be used to score a margin on the leather edge (Fig. 8), or to step off spaces (Fig. 10). Fig. 11 shows the use of the four-pronged thonging chisel. Always put one prong in the last hole cut, thus insuring even spacing throughout. Figs 12 and 13 show the use of the space maker and the revolving punch.

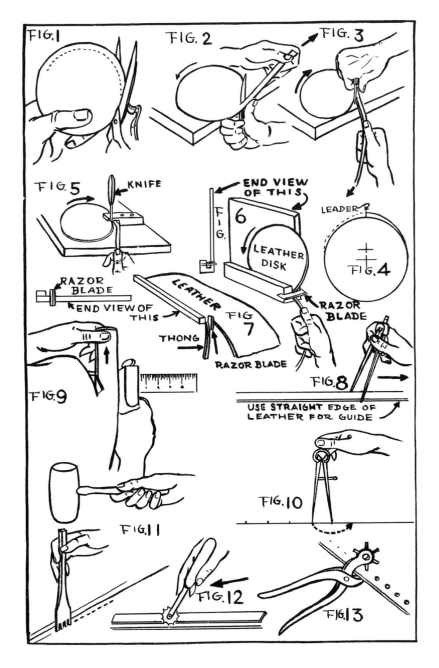

FIG. 1

FIG. 2

FIG. 3

FIG. 5   KNIFE

END VIEW OF THIS

LEADER

F I G. 6

LEATHER DISK

FIG. 4

RAZOR BLADE

END VIEW OF THIS

LEATHER

THONG

FIG 7

RAZOR BLADE

RAZOR BLADE

FIG. 9

FIG. 8

USE STRAIGHT EDGE OF LEATHER FOR GUIDE

FIG. 10

FIG. 11

FIG. 12

FIG. 13

PLATE 2—Thong Cutting.

5

PLATE 3

Two-Thong Flat Braid—Flat braiding is a systematic operation of alternately working from one side to the other. If the right-hand thong is carried to the left, over another and under another, the same thing is done next time with the left-hand thong, to the right.

Braiding can be done with from two thongs to an infinite number. However, the highest practicable number with which to work seems to be twenty-one thongs. That, at least, will constitute the maximum used in this book.

Some braiders advocate moistening the thongs and braiding them while damp. This system is very good for the experienced braider, but for the beginner, who might have to tear his braid apart and start over again, it is best first to work with his thongs dry, so that they will not be spoiled for possible rebraiding.

However, all thongs should be thoroughly saddle-soaped, and the lather rubbed in well. Then, even when dry, they will work easily and the braid can be closed up snugly. An even tension in the braid is important. Try to exert the same amount of pull on each thong and the braid will be uniform throughout.

The first braid will be a two-thong braid, similar to the common so-called chain-knot. Double the thong, place the loop over a peg and then tie an overhand knot as indicated in Fig. 1.

Bring the end, B, up through the knot, as demonstrated in Fig. 2. The bight of A is next pushed down through the loop formed by B as illustrated in Fig. 3.

For purposes of clarity the braid is not shown tightened in the drawing. But the next step in Fig. 3 is to pull thong B until it is fairly tight around the loop of A.

Bring the bight of thong B down through the bight of A and pull the end of A until it is tight around the bight of B (Fig. 4). Bring the bight of A through the bight of B and tighten by pulling on B, then the bight of B through A and so on, alternating until the length desired has been braided.

In this braid both the flesh side and the hair side of the leather alternately appears, one being the edge scallop and other the center portion.

Two one-foot lengths of ⅛ inch thongs will make about three inches in actual braid.

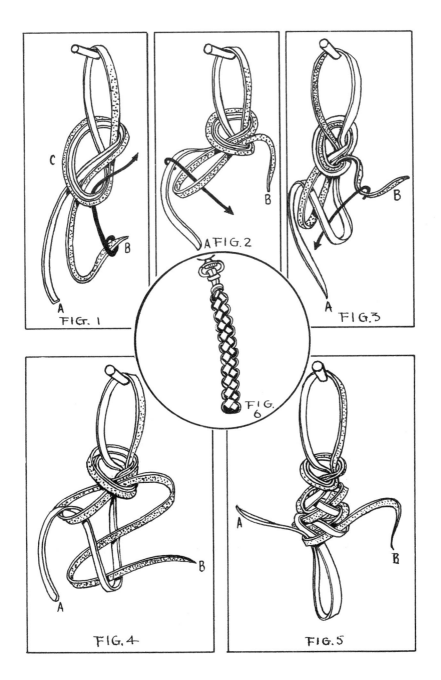

C

A FIG. 2

FIG. 1

B

B

A FIG. 3

FIG. 6

B

A

FIG. 4

A

B

FIG. 5

PLATE 3—Two-Thong Flat Braid.

7

PLATE 4

THREE-THONG HAIR BRAID—This braid is known as the "hair braid" and is one of the simplest and most commonly used of the flat braids. As a general rule it is dismissed, because of its simplicity, with the assumption that everyone knows how to do it. This is not true, and from our standpoint, it is most important that it be done correctly, as it is the key to more complicated flat braids.

As in the majority of flat braids the extreme right and left-hand thongs are worked alternately toward the center. They follow a definite sequence, in this case, of over one, under one.

In all braiding there is a length shrinkage which varies from approximately one-half to one-quarter of the original length. In the case of a three-strand braid, three $\frac{1}{8}$ inch thongs of one foot each shrink to ten inches of braid. Figuring on a one-quarter shrinkage would be a good average. Be sure the braiding is snug.

In the beginning, take the extreme left-hand thong, A (Fig. 1), and pass it over thong B; then take the extreme right-hand thong C and pass it over A (Fig. 2). Now bring B to the right, over C (Fig. 3). Bring A from the right toward the left over B (Fig. 4). In the next step, pass thong C from the left to the right over thong A; then thong B from the right to the left and over thong C. The thongs are now in their original position, thus completing one phase of the braid. To continue the braid, repeat as before.

FOUR-THONG BRAID—First cross the two center thongs (Fig. 5), C over B. Bring thong D to the left under B and thong A to the right over C and under D (Fig. 6). Now bring B to the left under A, and C to the right over D and under B. Next bring A to the left under C and bring D from the left to the right over B and under A (Fig. 7).

It is best in the beginning to place on the ends of the thongs the letters corresponding to those used here, as indicated in Fig. 5. Follow instructions carefully.

Shrinkage is approximately one-fourth of the original length.

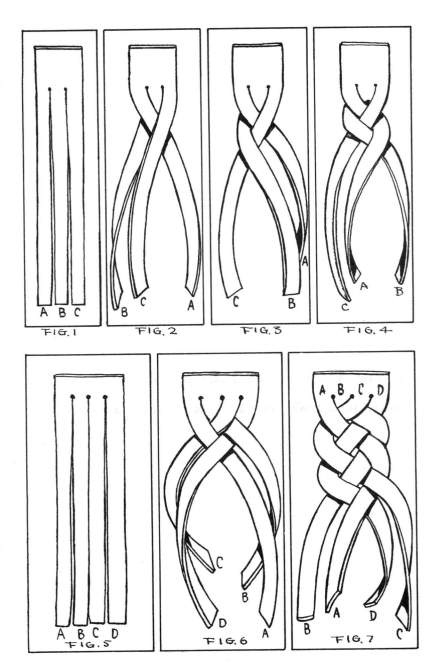

PLATE 4—Top: Three-Thong Hair Braid.
Bottom: Four-Thong Braid.

9

PLATE 5

THREE-PART INSIDE OR TRICK BRAID—This is an ordinary three part "hair braid" but it is worked inside; that is, the ends of the thongs are not free and are split from one single strap. It is tricky to make and mystifying to the uninitiated.

Lay the strap out in three equal parts and split it the desired length, leaving both ends closed, remembering that there is some shrinkage when the braid is complete, and the strap used in making a belt, for instance, should be nearly one-third longer than the desired length of the belt.

At the ends of the slits punch holes with the smallest tube on the revolving punch. This is to keep the leather from splitting further. Now dampen the leather by saddle-soaping it thoroughly as it is well to braid it while damp.

The first two steps are indicated in Fig. 2. Starting with the right-hand thong, C, place its bight over the center thong, B, then place the bight of the left-hand thong, A, over C. It will be noticed that a reverse or compensating braid is formed at the bottom. This bottom braid must be raveled out, while the top part remains intact.

To make the bottom braid disappear pass the entire bottom of the strap through the opening indicated in Fig. 2. This twists and tangles the thongs as in Fig. 3. The back part or flesh side of the strap will be forward and this should be twisted from left to right until the front side is foremost as in Fig. 4.

Meantime, as shown in Fig. 4, the braiding is continued and thong B is placed over thong A and thong C over thong B. The entire bottom of the strap now is passed through the opening shown in Fig. 4, and when straightened out, the whole work assumes an orderly appearance as in Fig. 5.

In this braid the moves have been made as simple as possible. That is, the bottom end is passed through the braid after each two moves. A "move" is the crossing of a thong over or under another.

In continuing the braid from its status in Fig. 5, place thong C over thong B, then thong A over thong C. Pass through the corresponding opening as was done in Fig. 2. Continue, or repeat, the moves shown in Figs. 3 and 4.

This braid should be made very tight at the top, so that when within a couple of inches of the bottom the braid becomes difficult to continue, the tightness in the upper part can be worked out and the braid distributed evenly throughout.

This braid is popular in making belts. It is also used for camera and shoulder bag straps, handles for quirts and crops and for bridle reins and wrist-watch straps. Be sure the original strap is a third longer than necessary, to absorb the shrinkage when it is braided.

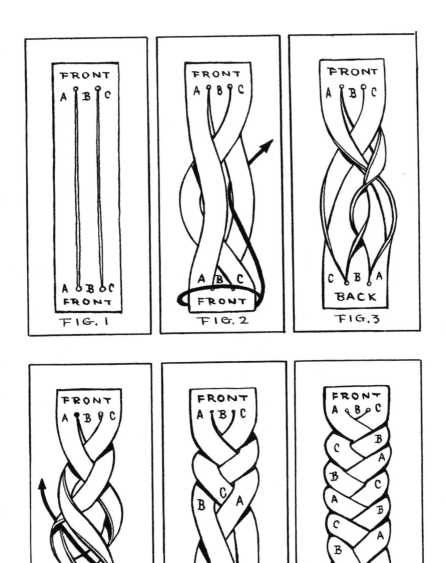

PLATE 5—Three-Part Inside or Trick Braid.

11

PLATE 6

FIVE-PART INSIDE TRICK BRAID—The five-part inside trick braid gives a pleasing effect of an over-two-and-under-two sequence. First cut a leather strap as shown in Fig. 1, being sure that the thongs are of equal width.

There is some shrinkage when the strap is braided and allowance must be made for this. For instance, in a strap 1¼ inches wide and eight inches long, cut into five ¼ inch thongs, the shrinkage will be about one inch.

The first step is shown in Fig. 2. Bring the bight of the extreme left-hand thong, A, to the right over thongs B and C. Then take the bight of the extreme right-hand thong, E, and bring it to the left over D and A, (Fig. 3). Now bring thong B on the extreme left over C and E to the right (Fig. 4), and pass thong D from right to left over A and B (Fig. 5).

In Fig. 6 two sequences are shown. First pass thong C on the extreme left to the right over thongs E and D. The upper portion of this braid must be held intact, and it will be seen that there have been five different passes. Next, take the bottom of the strap and pass the entire end through the opening between thongs C and D.

The braid should now look like the illustration in Fig. 7. Pay no attention to the tangled condition of the thongs at the bottom and continue to work at the top.

Take thong A on the extreme right and bring it to the left over thongs B and C (Fig. 8). Repeat this operation from each side four more times before the braid is turned from the bottom. For instance, bring the right thong and then the left thong to the center alternately, doing this five times with each thong.

The upper portion of the braid should now appear as in Fig. 9. Take the bottom of the strap shown in Fig. 9 and pass it through the part, as indicated, between thongs C and D. This lower part of the braid will then straighten itself out. Upon examining the top part, which must be held in place while the lower part is passed through, it will be apparent that there are exactly ten steps—that is, the right and left outer strands have been passed inward ten times.

The secret of this braid is that five passes are made each time before the bottom is turned.

When the braid reaches the point illustrated in Fig. 10 begin all over again. Pass thong A over B and C as was done in Fig. 1. When the point corresponding to that in Fig. 6 is reached, turn in the bottom as before. Then continue as in Fig. 7 until the end.

To make it easier to work at the bottom tighten up the braid at the top more than seems necessary. When the braid is completed loosen it until it is even throughout.

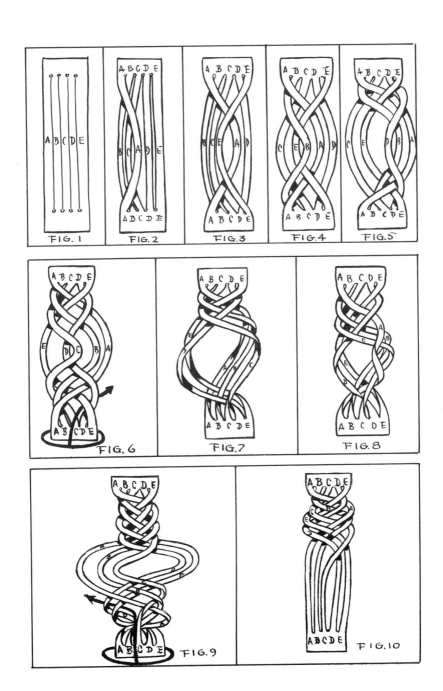

FIG. 1   FIG. 2   FIG. 3   FIG. 4   FIG. 5

FIG. 6   FIG. 7   FIG. 8

FIG. 9   FIG. 10

PLATE 6—Five-Part Inside Trick Braid.

13

PLATE 7

FIVE-THONG BRAIDS—To make the five-thong braid in Figs. 1, 2 and 3, first arrange the thongs as in Fig. 1. Now bring thong C, on the left, to the center over thongs D and E as in Fig. 2. Next bring thong B, on the extreme right, to the center over thongs A and C. Continue braiding first with the outer left thong and then the outer right one. In each instance they pass over two thongs. This makes an attractive herringbone braid.

Next we come to the braid shown in Figs. 4 and 5. The first step is to arrange the thongs as shown in Fig. 4. Start working with thong B on the extreme left and pass it to the center over thong E; then bring thong D on the extreme right to the left toward the center, over thong C, under thong A and over B, as illustrated in Fig. 5. In the next step bring thong E in Fig. 5 to the center by passing it over thong D and under thong C. Continue this braid by working alternately from left to right and right to left. This is an over-one-under-one sequence, so one thong is never passed over or under more than once.

Figs. 6 and 7 show another variation of the five-thong flat braid. In this case it will be noticed that the center thong, C, becomes a sort of core and runs straight down the center of the braid.

The first step is to arrange the thongs as shown in Fig. 6. It will be noticed that thongs A and E, the two outer thongs, always pass under thong C, but alternate in passing over and under each other. In the case of thongs F and D, they always pass over thong C and alternate in passing over and under each other.

Starting with Fig. 6, take thong D in the right hand and pass it beneath thong A and over thong C. Take thong B on the left and pass it toward the right under thong E and over thong D, at the juncture of D and C. Thong B thus passes over both D and C. Now on the right, thong A is brought to the left over thong B and under thong C. From the left, thong E is brought to the right over thong D and under thong A, at the junction of A and C. Thus E passes under both A and C.

This offers a fine opportunity to use thongs of different colors, or at least to make thong C different from the others.

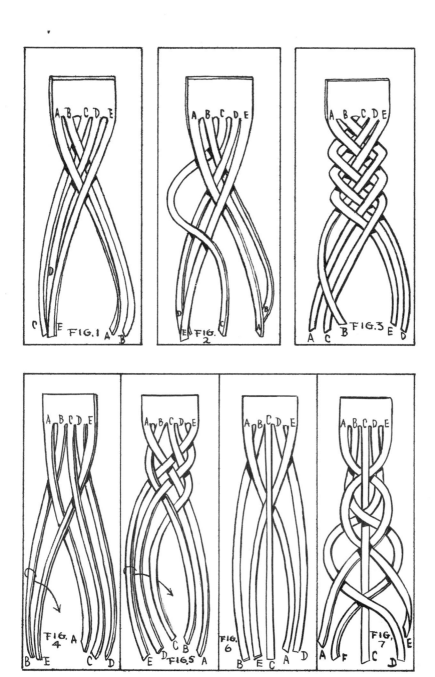

PLATE 7—Five-Thong Braids.

15

PLATE 8

Six-Thong Braids—The first of the braids of six thongs will be the over-one-under-one braid. To begin, arrange the thongs as in Fig. 1. This is done by crossing the two middle thongs, with thong C brought to the right over thong D. Then bring thong B to the right, under D and follow by bringing thong E to the left over C and under B.

Now alternate first on the left-hand side and then on the right, always working the outer thong to the center. Thus, in Fig. 2, thong A is moved over D and under E, and then from the right, thong F is moved under C, over B and under A.

Keep the braid snug and be sure there are an equal number of thongs on each side. When there are four on a side, work the thong on that side, as in Fig. 3. The next move is to bring thong C over B, under A and over D.

Another example of the six-thong flat braid is shown in Figs. 4 and 5. Arrange the thongs as shown in Fig. 4, which is done by moving thong A on the extreme left, to the right, under thongs B and C to the center; then moving thong F on the extreme right over to the left by passing it over thongs E and D and under A.

In this braid the extreme left-hand thong will always pass under two toward the center; the extreme right-hand thong will always pass over two and under one toward the center. Keep the braided part pushed up snugly.

This makes an attractive braid and when finished it will be seen that its sequence is under-two-over-one from the left side, and over-two-under-one from the right side.

The third example of six-thong braiding is somewhat different in that the extreme right-hand thong is used continually. It could just as well be the extreme left-hand thong, but in the illustration the right-hand one has been chosen.

First, as in Fig. 6, take thong F and move it to the extreme left by passing it under thong E, over D, under C, over B and under A. Then take thong E and carry it to the extreme left by passing it under thong D, over C, under B, over A, and under F. Keep the braid closed up snugly. Although the finished braid may seem at first to slant or incline to the left, it will soon straighten out.

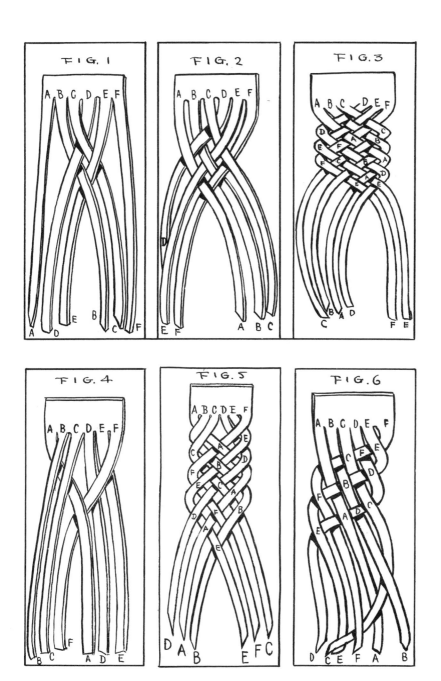

PLATE 8—Six-Thong Braids.

17

PLATE 9

Six-Thong Braid—Special attention should be paid to the making of this braid as it furnishes the key to the more intricate and beautiful types of double braids to follow—especially those of nine, thirteen and twenty-one thongs.

Arrange the thongs as shown in Fig. 1. Bring thong A on the extreme left to the right over thong B and thongs C and D. Bring thong F on the extreme right to the left over thongs E and A.

Move thong B to the right by passing it under thong C and over thongs D and F (Fig. 2). It will be noticed in the drawing, which shows the braiding loose so the course of the individual thongs may better be followed, that thong B is under A as well as under C. This may appear to be wrong but it is not; it is thus that the braid is made double. Take thong E on the extreme right, bring it toward the left to the center by passing it under thongs A and B. In this instance it will be noted that E already was under thong F and now it is under all three thongs F, A and B.

The next step in Fig. 3 reveals further how this braid is made. Now thong C, on the extreme left, is passed over thong D and under thongs F and E. On the right, thong A is passed over B and C.

In referring to the first step in Fig. 1, observe that in working from the left side, the outer thong A first passes over one and then under two. In Fig. 2, the extreme left thong B passes under one and over two, and now in Fig. 3 it passes over one and under two.

On the right-hand side, too, it will be noted that in Fig. 1 the extreme right-hand thong E passes over two; then in Fig. 2 thong E passes under two and in Fig. 3 the extreme right hand thong A passes over two.

This is the key. Each time alternate on each side. When the first thong on the left is passed *over* one time, it is passed *under* the next time. And the same is true on the right-hand side. When tightened, the braid will be relatively narrower than other six-thong braids but it will be double, as indicated in a side view in Fig. 4.

Seven-Thong Braid—In this braid begin with thong D over thong E; thong B under C and E; thong G to the left over F and under D and B. Pass thong A to the right over C and under E and G. Now pass F to the left over D and under B and A. Continue as in Fig. 5, with each outer thong passing over one and under two.

Nine-Thong Braid—In this braid divide the thongs with four on the left and five on the right. Start by bringing E over D to the left. This can be followed by the drawing. Notice that this braid has an over-one-under-one sequence in the center, but under two each time on both edges.

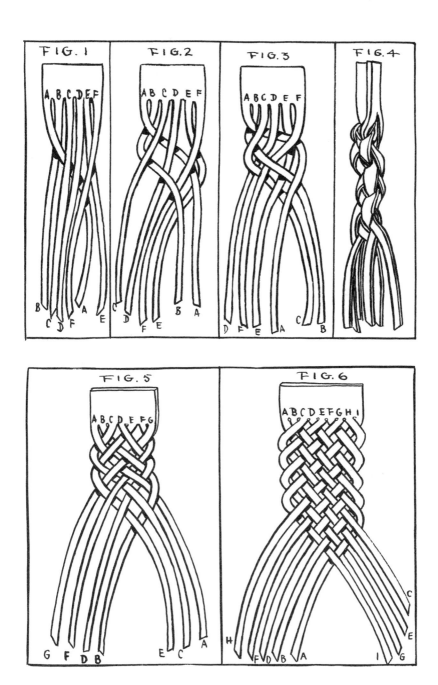

PLATE 9—Six, Seven and Nine-Thong Braids.

19

PLATE 10

THIRTEEN-THONG BRAID—This and the braid to follow are the most beautiful of the flat braids. The key to both may be found in the braid of six thongs in Plate 8. Always remember to alternate over and under on each side; for instance when the thongs are passed *over* on one side, they are passed *under* on this side the next time.

Divide the thongs seven on the left side and six on the right. As each thong is worked from the outside it comes only to the center.

Begin with thong 4 and pass it to the right over thongs 5 and 6, and under 7. Then pass thong 9 to the left under 8 and 4. Take thong 3 to the right over 5 and under 6, 7 and 9. Bring thong 11 on the right to the left under 10, 8 and 4, and over 3. Pass thong 2 on the left to the right under 5 and 6 and over 7, 9 and 11. Bring the extreme right-hand thong 13, to the left over 12, under 10, over 8, under 4, over 3 and under 2.

This preliminary, which appears somewhat intricate, is not absolutely necessary, but it closes the braid at the top so there is no loss of leather.

Now, take strand 1 on the extreme left and pass it over 5, 6 and 7, and under 9, 11 and 13.

On the right, take thong 12 and bring it to the left under 10, 8 and 4 and over 3, 2 and 1. The extreme left-hand thong is now No. 5. Previously the extreme left-hand thong No. 1, was passed *over* the three nearest it. Now alternate—and this is the secret of the double braid—by passing it *under* the three nearest—that is, 6, 7 and 9, and *over* 11, 13 and 12. On the extreme right, bring the outer thong, No. 10, to the left center by passing it *over* (the one before on this side went *under*) 8, 4 and 3 and *under* 2, 1 and 5.

On the left pass over three and under three to the right center. On the right pass under three and over three to the center. The braid is consistent from now on. Remember to alternate the passes on each side. Keep the braid snug and the thongs in order.

By placing the thongs in a drawer and closing it upon them at the beginning they can be kept side by side. If necessary use paper clips and small pieces of paper and attach each number to the thong.

FLAT BRAID OF TWENTY-ONE THONGS—The principle outlined above is carried out in the twenty-one thong braid, (Fig. 2). Divide the thongs with eleven on the left and ten on the right. To avoid confusion from the start, bring thong 1 on the extreme left to the right center by passing it over the nearest five and under the next five. Then from the right, bring No. 21 to the left center by passing it under five and over five. Next on the left pass under five and over five and so on.

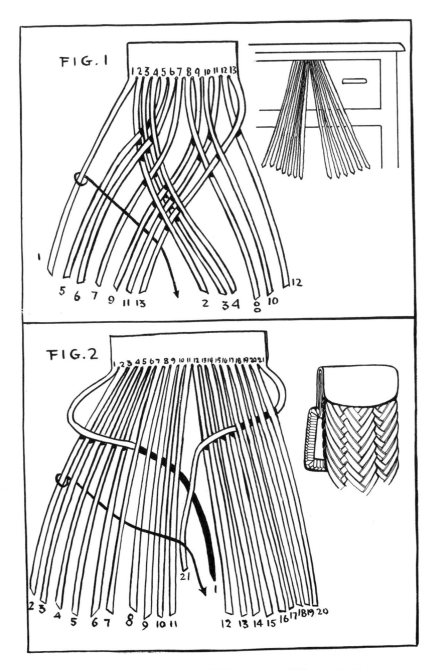

FIG. 1

1 2 3 4 5 6 7 8 9 10 11 12 13

1

5 6 7 9 11 13   2 3 4 8 10   12

FIG. 2

1 2 3 4 5 6 7 8 9 10 11 12 13 14 15 16 17 18 19 20 21

21   1

2 3 4 5 6 7 8 9 10 11   12 13 14 15 16 17 18 19 20

PLATE 10—Thirteen and Twenty-one Thong Braids.

21

PLATE 11

The Conquistador Braid—Here is a remarkable braid which was used by the old time Conquistadores on their sword belts and seems to have been lost somewhere along the line. It is made with one thong. Be sure this thong is of consistent thickness as the braid will not be regular if the thong is thin in some spots and thick in others.

Start with four holes or slits in the leather, evenly spaced and about ⅛ inch from the end. Hold the dress or hair side of the leather toward you with holes upward. Pass the thong through the hole on the left to the back, leaving a small portion of it on the near side, as in Fig. 1. Bring it back to the front and pass it again through the same hole to the rear. Draw it tight, anchoring the end, and bring it forward and pass it through the second hole from front to rear as shown in Fig. 2.

Pass the thong through the third hole (Fig. 3) and then through the fourth hole (Fig. 4). Make the thongs snug.

Introduce the fid under the bight, as in Fig. 5, from the left side upward to the right. Then bring the thong over to the front and draw it through this opening, as in Fig. 6. Draw it up snug, always using as nearly as possible the same amount of pressure on each thong. This will keep the braid consistent throughout.

The next step is shown in Fig. 7, where the thong has passed under the bight of the thong in hole No. 3 and to the rear of itself. The fid already has prepared the next bight to receive the working end of the thong. Continue until the thong has been passed through all four bights. Now start back to the right by passing under the newly formed bight in the second row, as shown in Fig. 8. Figure 9 illustrates a continuance of the sequence. Continue until the thong has passed through all four bights.

Now start back to the left. Thus it goes from left to right, and right to left until the braid is of the desired length. Finish it off by introducing it into four holes of another strap. This makes a fine belt or wrist strap for a watch.

The finished braid is shown in Fig. 10. At first there will be a give to this braid and it may seem elastic. But after it has been worn it will remain at the point to which it has stretched and will no longer be resilient. So allow a little for the give, depending on how tightly the braid has been made.

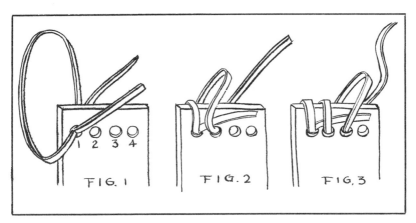

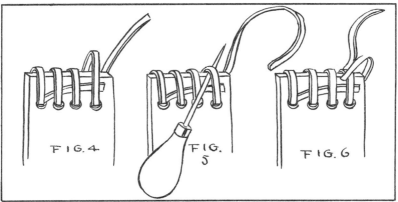

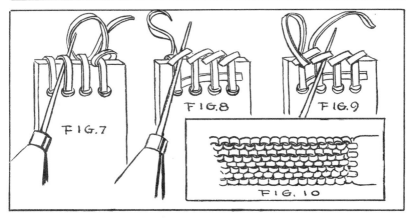

PLATE 11—The Conquistador Braid.

23

PLATE 12

SLIT BRAIDS—By slitting the leather and passing it back through the holes alternately, the effect of a braid is obtained, although it is not a true braid in the usual sense.

An example of this braid may be found in attaching a buckle to a strap. First punch out in the middle of the strap the slot through which the tongue of the buckle goes and introduce the buckle, as shown in Fig. 1. The flesh sides on each portion of the strap face each other.

Make a vertical slit as shown, and indicated as 1, less than the width of the strap itself. Make slit No. 4 in the other part of the strap a little below; then slits 2, 5, and 3. These should be stair-stepped as indicated.

Bring up that portion of the strap indicated as A and pull it through slit 1 from the rear to the front. Then pull the portion shown as B through slit 4 also from the rear to the front. Now again pull A through from the rear to the front. Continue to the end. Don't pull the straps through the slits sideways. Work with the leather damp after it has been thoroughly saddle-soaped.

Fig. 2 shows leather or metal conchas as they are fastened to cowboy bridles and saddles by this method.

Fig. 3 illustrates a practical application of the various flat braids in making a belt. The braiding starts from the end in which the belt holes are punched, indicated by D. The loose ends are secured in that portion shown as A. Before the braid is sewn in, however, introduce the buckle and the belt loop, illustrated in C. One type of belt loop made from a Turk's Head or woven knot is shown as B. The method of making this will be shown later.

Fig. 4 shows how the three-thong inside braid (Plate 5) can be used as a belt, and in this case there are no loose ends to cover or sew in. The five-thong inside braid (Plate 6) also makes a good belt, and either of these braids may be used as wrist loops on whips and quirts.

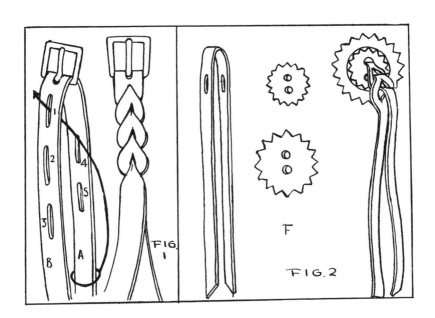

FIG. 1

FIG. 2

F

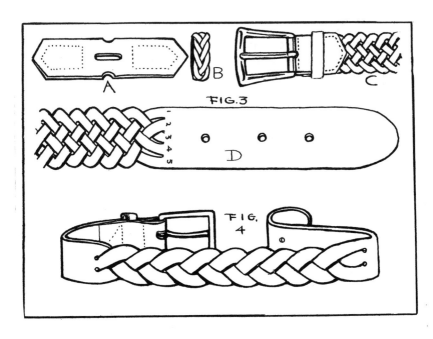

FIG. 3

A   B   C

FIG. 4

D

PLATE 12—Slit Braids.

25

PLATE 13

ROUND BRAIDS OF ONE THONG OR TWIST BRAID—This valuable type of braiding—for while it may not appear to be braiding, it is considered as such by the Spanish Trenzadores—has been greatly neglected. It is simple and has many applications.

Take a leather strap or thong which is uniformly thick throughout and wet it thoroughly; however, it should not be so wet that moisture appears when you press it with your finger.

Do not actually twist the leather but roll it upon itself, the flesh side in (Fig. 1). Keep rolling it until it is a hollow tube and then begin gradually to stretch it until the tube narrows and the leather comes together at the spiral lines. While it is still damp, holding the two ends so that the roll does not uncurl, roll it beneath your foot or upon some hard surface with a piece of wood.

The two ends should then be clamped or nailed down to a board and the leather allowed to dry completely. It will retain its twist or roll. The ends may be left flat and attached to boxes for handles, or as shown in Fig. 2, inserted in holes and nailed or fastened inside.

With a strap about one inch or more in width according to the size of the twist you wish, you can make a sports belt. Leave a sufficient portion flat at both ends—at one for attaching the buckle and at the other for punching holes.

ROUND BRAID OF TWO THONGS OR TRICK TWIST—This may not be new but I worked it out in the following manner: Slit the leather down the center, leaving the two ends closed as in Fig. 3. Dampen the leather, and then, with the hair side toward you, bring one end through to the front, as shown in Fig. 4. Continue pulling the bottom end through from rear to front until the braid is tight and then pull straight.

This braid can be made into a belt, or, by using a small piece of leather, into a wrist-watch band, as shown in Fig. 7.

Don't forget to provide for the usual shrinkage—about ½ inch in a wrist-watch strap.

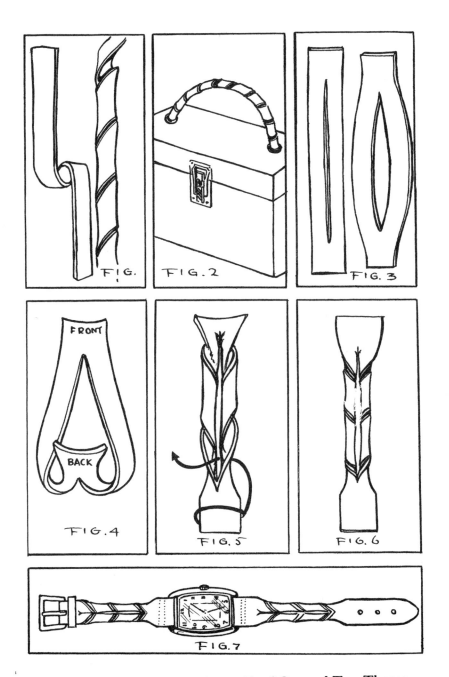

FIG. 1   FIG. 2   FIG. 3

FRONT

BACK

FIG. 4   FIG. 5   FIG. 6

FIG. 7

PLATE 13—Round and Twist Braids of One and Two Thongs.

27

PLATE 14

ROUND BRAID OF FOUR THONGS—The four-thong round braid is made with or without a core. When using a core, which may be rope, rounded leather or any desirable round object, arrange the thongs as in Fig. 1. The combined width of the thongs should be the same as the circumference of the core. If the core measures one inch around, each thong should be ¼ of an inch in width.

Very thin leather may be used in this type of covering, as the leather is subjected to no strain when in use. If thick leather is used, it is well to bevel the edge on the flesh side so that the braid will lie snug.

Some braiders work with their thongs thoroughly damp. I usually saddle-soap the thongs and allow them to dry. In working with damp thongs the pulling often stretches the leather and the thongs get narrower as they proceed downward.

In Fig. 1 the two thongs in front are crossed, bringing thong 1 to the right over thong 2, and carrying thong 2 toward the left.

Bring thong 4 around to the rear, following the path shown in the arrow-line in Fig. 1. Fig. 2 shows thong 4 on the left, having passed beneath thong 3 and over thong 1.

The arrow-line in Fig. 2 shows the path of thong 3. Bring it around to the rear and back again to the front, passing under thong 2 and over thong 4 (Fig. 3).

Thong 2 is worked next. It follows the course of the arrow-line in Fig. 3, going around the rear and back to the front under thong 1 and over thong 3.

There are always two thongs on each side. Work alternately with the outer or upper ones, passing to the rear and following the sequence of under one thong and over the next.

Keep the braid carefully closed up as the work progresses. Unless the same amount of pull is used on each thong, it will show in the finished braid.

Continue to the end as shown in Figs. 4 and 5. Then tie down the thongs.

When the braid is completed, saddle-soap it thoroughly and roll it under your foot on the floor or some other hard surface. Don't be afraid to exert a little pressure as this will smooth down the braid and bring it closer together.

Cowboys often smooth and polish braid that is made without a core (Figs. A, B, C and D) by drawing it through a series of holes in hard wood or bone, each hole being smaller than the previous one, with the sharp edges of the holes beveled.

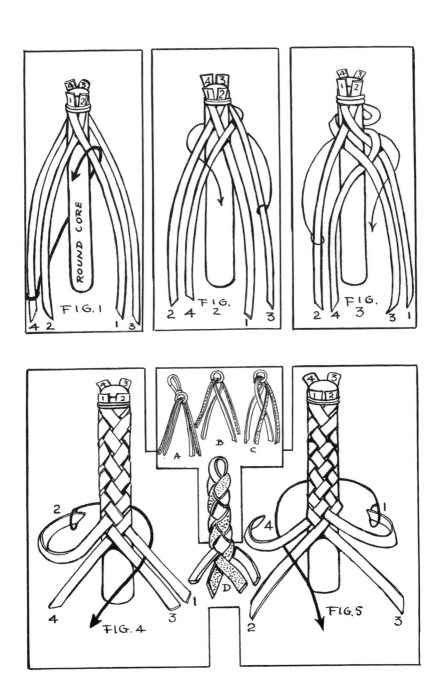

PLATE 14—Round Braid of Four Thongs.

29

PLATE 15

TURK'S HEAD TERMINAL FOR ROUND BRAID—There are cases where it may be desirable to finish off a round braid with a handsome knot, instead of merely tying it down. It is then that the Turk's Head Terminal Knot is used.

When a core has been braided over, continue the braid beyond the core and then arrange it so that the thongs appear as in Fig. 1.

Pass thong 1 around the rear as shown in Fig. 2 and turn thong 3 so that the flesh side is toward you. Thong 1 should also be turned so the flesh is toward you as in Fig. 3.

Lash the thongs together in this order and turn the ends upward to make the braiding easier (Fig. 4). The thongs are now separated as shown in Fig. 5, with the flesh sides of all of them upward.

Fold thong 2 over thong 4, leaving a bight in 2 near the spot where it is lashed, as shown in Fig. 6. Then fold thong 4 over both thongs 2 and 1, also leaving a bight in thong 4, as shown in Fig. 7.

Pass thong 1 over thong 4 and thong 3. Then thrust thong 3 over thong 1 and through the bight in thong 2 as indicated by the arrow-line in Fig. 8. The thongs are now arranged as pictured in Fig. 9. The hair or smooth sides of all are upward.

Continuing in the same direction, which in this case is counterclockwise, pass thong 1 around and to the outside of the bight of thong 2 and up under thong 2 and thong 3. This thong emerges in the center of the braid as indicated by the arrow-line in Fig. 10 and shown in Fig. 11.

Pass thong 4 around and outside of the bight of thong 3 and then up through the center, under thong 3 and thong 1. Next move thong 2 in the same fashion and finally thong 3. Work the knot tight but be sure to press it back on the braid or it will be inclined to slip upward.

The protruding thongs may be cut off close to the knot or trimmed evenly and left. Saddle-soap the knot, mould it gently and it will remain in this shape after it dries.

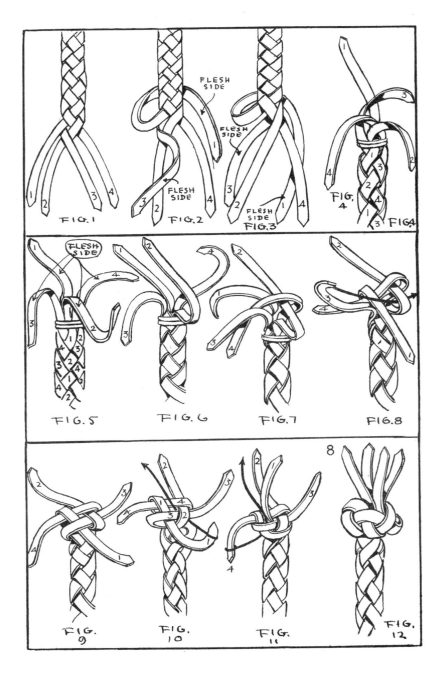

PLATE 15—Turk's Head Terminal For Round Braid.

31

PLATE 16

ROUND BRAID OF SIX THONGS—It is not practicable to employ a round braid of more than four thongs without a core. Therefore, in making the round braid of six thongs, a core is used. This may be a rope, rounded leather or other material, or possibly a hard twisted rawhide core such as that used in riding crops and other whips.

The combined width of the thongs should be the same as the circumference of the object to be covered.

Arrange the thongs as shown in Fig. 1. This is to be a braid in which the sequence is over one thong, under one thong and over the next, or what is usually termed the basket-weave.

In making this braid there are always three thongs on one side and three on the other.

First bring thong 2 to the left and over thong 1, inclining thong 1 to the right.

Bring thong 4, which belongs to the right-hand group, around to the rear over thong 5, under thong 6 and over thong 2, to return to its original side, as indicated by the arrow-line in Fig. 1 and shown in Fig. 2.

Pass thong 5 around to the rear and to the front where it goes over thong 3, under thong 1 and over thong 4, to return to its original left-hand side.

Continue the braid in the same manner to the desired length, always working with the extreme left-hand or extreme right-hand thong. Remember—to the rear, then to the front and over one, under one and over one.

Another method of braiding with six thongs is shown beginning with Fig. 7. Here, as before, the thongs are grouped three on a side.

First cross thong 2 to the left over thong 1. Then bring thong 5 forward under thong 6 and over thong 2, indicated in the arrow-line in Fig. 7 and shown in Fig. 8.

Bring thong 4 forward under thong 3, and over both thongs 1 and 5 (Fig. 8). Now start working the thongs around the rear.

Bring thong 3 on the right around the rear and forward on the left under thongs 6 and 2 and over thong 4 and return to its original side, as indicated by the arrow-line in Fig. 9 and shown in Fig. 10.

On the left, bring thong 6 around the rear and forward to the right under thong 1 and over thongs 5 and 3 (Fig. 10).

Remember that in this braid the thongs on the right pass around back and to the front *under* two and *over* one, while those on the left pass around and *under* one and *over* two. Continue this sequence until the end. The finished braid is shown in Fig. 13.

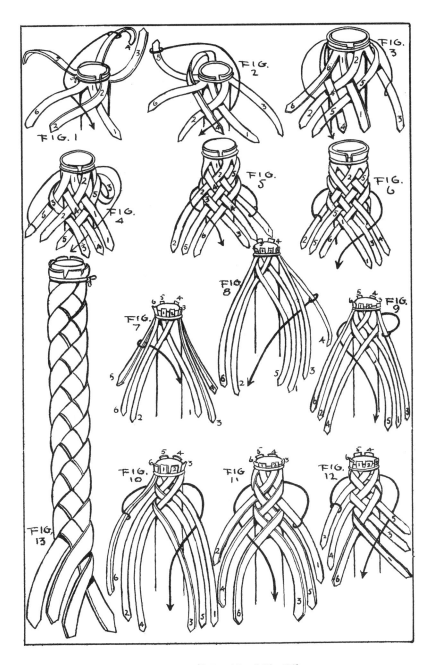

PLATE 16—Round Braid of Six Thongs.

33

PLATE 17

HERRINGBONE BRAID OF EIGHT THONGS—For the eight-thong herringbone braid, fasten the thongs at the top of the core as indicated in Fig. 1. When working with so many thongs it is difficult to space them around the core. The best way to do this is first to lash down thong 1 and pass the thread or string completely around the core; then place thong 3 in position and pass the thread over it and around the core; then thong 5, and so on. Another method is to apply some fast-drying cement around the core at this point, attach the thongs and finally tie them down.

Divide the thongs so that there are four on the right-hand side and four on the left-hand side. In these illustrations, those on the right are indicated by even numbers and those on the left by odd numbers.

Bring thong 7 of the left-hand group around the rear and to the front, under thongs 8 and 6, over thongs 4 and 2 and back on its original side. This is shown in Fig. 1 and the course of thong 8 is also indicated by the arrow-line. This thong goes around the rear and back to the front under thongs 5 and 3 and over thongs 1 and 7.

The sequence is always the same in this braid. Bring the rearmost thong on either side around the core, under two and over two.

In Fig. 2, thong 8 is shown in position and the arrow-line indicates the path of thong 5 on the other side. It goes to the rear and then forward on the right-hand side under thongs 6 and 4 and over thongs 8 and 2.

Follow the diagrams and by way of practice, number the thongs as shown and check the work by the diagrams, seeing that each thong rests in the place indicated.

Keep the braid up snug, saddle-soap it thoroughly when finished and roll it beneath the foot. When almost dry, polish with the heel of the hand, one of the best methods of brightening up leather. This is an attractive braid and is widely used on quirts, riding crops and other whips.

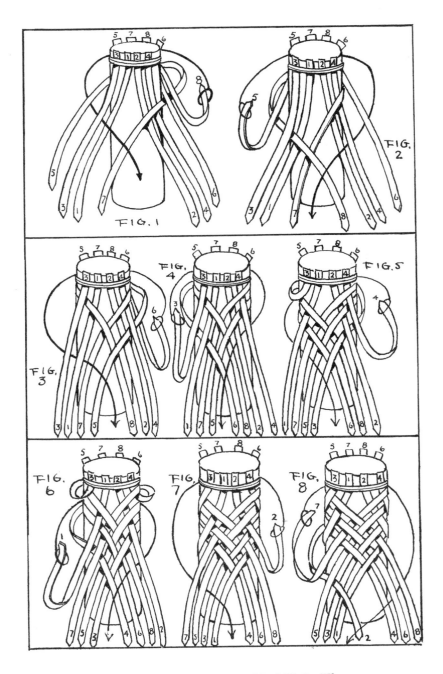

PLATE 17—Herringbone Braid of Eight Thongs.

35

PLATE 18

BACK BRAID OF SIX THONGS—First, make the foundation of this braid by braiding down with six thongs in a round braid of an over-one-under-one sequence. The braid should be made loosely, that is, the spaces between the thongs should be approximately the width of a thong.

When the skeleton braid is worked to the desired length, divide the thongs, with three on the right and three on the left. In Fig. 1 notice that where the two middle thongs cross, thong 4, which inclines to the right, crosses over thong 5, which inclines to the left.

Take the upper left-hand thong, No. 6 in this case, and pass it around to the rear, over the thong on the extreme right (No. 3), under the next (No. 1), and up alongside and to the right of No. 4. This thong will parallel No. 4 to the very top. (The move explained is indicated by the arrow-line in Fig. 1.)

Bring the next highest thong on the left (No. 3) around to the rear and under the one on the extreme right (No. 3) and up alongside and parallel to thong 1 (indicated by the arrow-line in Fig. 2). Bring the last thong on the left (No. 5) around and parallel with thong 3, passing under thong 6, as did No. 3 (indicated by the arrow-line in Fig. 3).

Fig. 4 shows these thongs in their proper positions.

In Fig. 5 the braid begins. Pass thong 4 to the right, over two thongs and under two thongs. As the sequence will be over-two-under-two, remember that from now on all working thongs will pass over two thongs and under two thongs.

In Fig. 6 the work is with thong 3, which passes up to the right, over two and under two. In Fig. 7, pass thong 1 which is on the right around to the rear and up in the same relationship as the previous two—over two, under two.

This will be the sequence to remember in passing the last three thongs on the right—always over two and under two, until they reach the top. Those on the left passed upwards parallel to the thongs on their left—those on the right in the over-two-under-two sequence.

Thus, although only six thongs are used, the equivalent of a twelve-thong braid is obtained.

To tighten this braid, start working down with those thongs which are fastened at the top and when the bottom is reached tighten them upwards. This gives a finished end at the bottom.

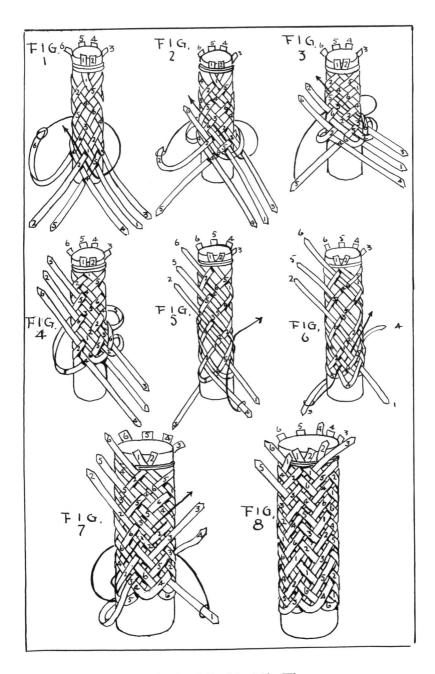

PLATE 18—Back Braid of Six Thongs.

37

PLATE 19

Back Braid of Eight Thongs—By braiding down the core with eight thongs in a basket-weave—over one, under one sequence—and then at the bottom braiding back up in an over two, under two sequence a sixteen-thong braid is obtained. The bottom presents a finished end which does not have to be covered.

Start by arranging the thongs as shown in Fig. 1. Begin the basket-weave by crossing thong 1 to the right over thong 2 and incline thong 2 to the left. Bring thong 7 around to the rear, under 8, over 6, under 4 and over 1, as indicated by the arrow-line in Fig. 1 and shown in Fig. 2.

From the right-hand group of thongs, take No. 8 and bring it to the rear under 5, over 3, under 2 and over 7, indicated by the arrow-line in Fig. 2 and shown in Fig. 3. Continue braiding down, first from one side and then the other, until the work has progressed to the point illustrated in Fig. 5, or in other words, until the desired length of the finished braid is reached. Leave a space between thongs just the width of a thong.

To begin the back braid, take thong 5 on the left, pass it to the rear and then forward under 6, over 4, under 7 and then up along the right side of thong 8, following exactly the same course as thong 8, which in the first step would bring it under No. 2. This is indicated in the arrow-line in Fig. 5 and shown in Fig. 6.

The other thongs on the left are braided accordingly as shown up to Fig. 9. Now, to begin the second phase of the back braid, bring thong 8 to the right, over 5 and 1, under 3 and 4, and over 2 and 6.

Note that the diagrams in Figs. 10, 11 and 12 show all the braiding crowded to the front. This is done merely to illustrate the work in greater detail; actually, the core is turned as you proceed.

Thong 1 is worked next (Fig. 10). Pass it over thongs 3 and 4, under 2 and 6 and over 7 and 8 (Fig. 11). Pass thong 4 over thongs 2 and 6, under 7 and 8 and over 1 and 4. Pass thong 6 over thongs 2 and 8, under 5 and 1, over 3 and 4, and so on.

The thongs working up toward the left, follow exactly the thongs to their left; those inclining up to the right maintain an individual over-two-under-two sequence.

To tighten this braid, begin at the top where the thongs are lashed down. Work down one set at a time—that is, those slanting downward to the right, and follow them back to the top. Then tighten those inclining to the left, all the way to the bottom and back to the top.

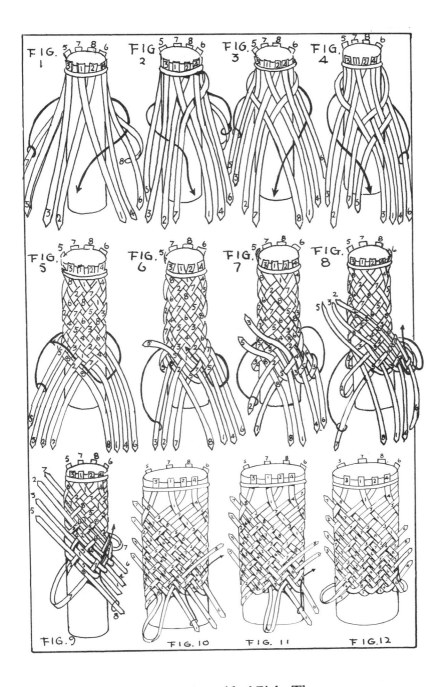

PLATE 19—Back Braid of Eight Thongs.

39

PLATE 20

Round Braid of Twelve Thongs—In making the round braid of twelve thongs, lash the thongs around the top of the core as shown in Fig. 1. The total width of the twelve thongs should be the same as the circumference of the core. In these drawings a little space is left between the thongs to make it easier to follow the process of braiding.

In this case the six thongs on the left are given the uneven numbers, 1 to 11 and those on the right are even, 2 to 12. Each thong will return to its own side, always advancing at each step from the thong in the rear to the one in the front of its group, or "going to the head of the class."

The braid is alternate—work first one side and then the next. The sequence is the same on both sides—over two thongs, under two thongs and over two thongs.

First, bring thong 11, the rearmost of the left-hand group, around to the rear, pass it over thongs 12 and 10, then under thongs 8 and 6 and finally over thongs 4 and 2, returning it to its side. This is shown in Fig. 1.

Also in Fig. 1 is indicated the path of the next thong—No. 12—from the right-hand side. Bring it to the rear, around and to the front, pass it over thongs 9 and 7, under thongs 5 and 3 and finally over thongs 1 and 11.

The next move is from the left side: Take thong 9 around to the rear and pass it over thongs 10 and 8, under thongs 6 and 4 and finally over thongs 2 and 12.

This is indicated by the arrow-line in Fig. 2 and shown in Fig. 3.

Continue this braid, working from the right side and then the left side, and follow the sequence of over two, under two and over two.

Fig. 7 shows the result, with the braid loosely woven, of arranging black or colored thongs on the left side. This gives a pleasing pattern. Other patterns may be worked out by using thongs of different colors, and alternating the colors on each side.

As the work progresses keep the braid snug and exert the same amount of pull on each thong. Saddle-soap thoroughly and roll beneath the foot until the braid has a smooth surface.

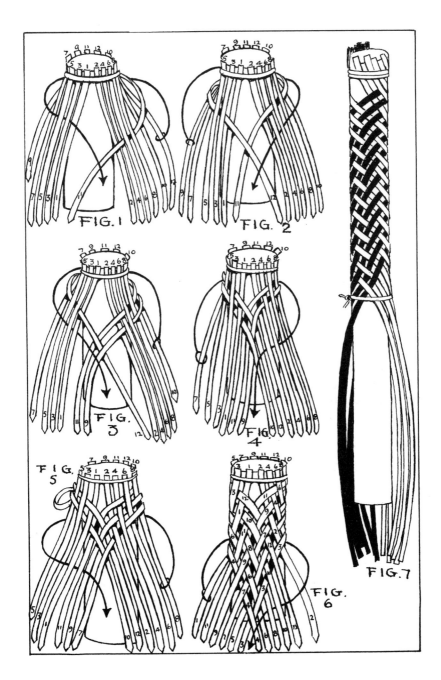

PLATE 20—Round Braid of Twelve Thongs.

41

PLATE 21

How to Make a Braided Quirt—The first step is to make
the core or filler of the quirt. Take a piece of leather, preferably
8-ounce leather, which is about 1/16 inch in thickness, and cut it
as shown in Fig. 1.

Dampen the leather thoroughly and nail the narrow end to a
piece of board as shown in Fig. 2. Roll or twist it in a clockwise
direction, so that the flesh side is innermost (Fig. 3). This type of
twist braid is demonstrated in Plate 13.

When the core has been twisted tightly, stretch it and then nail
the wide end to the board and leave it to dry (Fig. 4).

Next, make the wrist strap by braiding together three ⅛ inch
thongs (Figs. 6 and 7). Braid tightly, using the method illustrated
in Plate 4. Cut the lash, also of 8-ounce leather, with a horizontal
slit in the center (Fig. 10).

The core should be completely dry before covering. Cut off the
parts through which the nails have been driven. Insert a spike nail
in the top (Fig. 5) to stiffen the handle part. Cover this nail top
with a small strip of leather, bringing the ends down on the handle,
and lash them there. Next, attach the wrist strap, lashing it to the
sides of the top of the handle between the ends of the strips which
covered the head of the spike nail. Directly below the ends of the
wrist strap, lash the six ⅛ inch thongs which will be braided over
the entire core (Fig. 8).

The braid for the quirt is the six-thong back braid shown in
Plate 18. Carry the braid just a trifle beyond the end of the core
at the bottom before starting to braid it back. When the braid is
back at the top, lash it down and continue wrapping the twine
around the ends of the braid as well as around the ends of the wrist
strap, until a bulge is formed for the knob of the handle.

Cover this bulge with a Turk's Head made with ¼ inch thonging, a pattern for which is given in Fig. 12. Insert a sheet of carbon
paper underneath this pattern and over a piece of heavy brown
paper. Trace the pattern, transferring it to the brown paper. Cut
flush at the right-hand side and then roll up the paper so the lines
on both ends come together. Place pins in the loops marked with
an X. Lay the standing end of the thong at the point marked
starting point, and hold it there with a light rubber band. Then
follow the lines around with the working end, always passing *over*
each intersection of thongs except those marked with a *circle* in
which case pass *under.*

Remove the Turk's Head from the pattern by withdrawing the
pins, and tighten it over the knob on the handle. Dampen the
lash, insert the end of the quirt through the slit and then pass the
ends down through the center of the braid (Fig. 9) and pull tight.

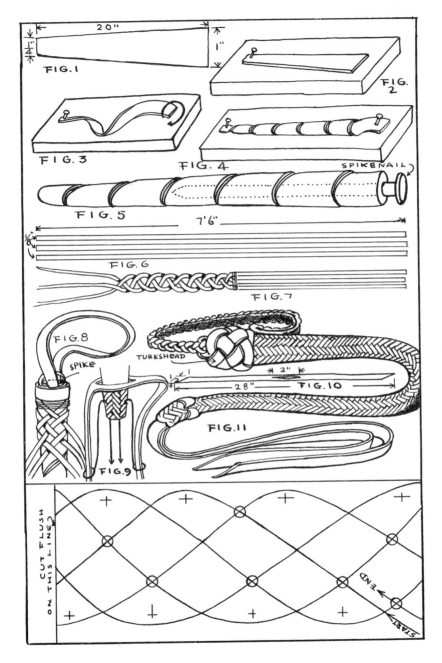

FIG.1

FIG. 2

FIG.3

FIG. 4

SPIKENAIL

FIG. 5

7'6"

FIG.6

FIG.7

FIG.8

SPIKE

TURKSHEAD

2"

28"

FIG.10

FIG.9

FIG.11

CUT FLUSH ON THIS LINE

START

END

PLATE 21—How to Make a Braided Quirt.

PLATE 22

Square Braid of Four-Thongs—This braid is made with four thongs but the same principle can be used with three, or with a greater number. It is based on the so-called Sailor's Crown Knot, and is used in making lanyards, watch fobs, dog leashes, and in covering quirt handles, as will be shown later.

Begin as in Fig. 1, showing two thongs of which both ends of each are used. Place the thongs so that the working ends are interlaced as illustrated. The white thong shows end B at the left and end B1 at the right. The black thong shows end A at the top and end A1 at the bottom.

Fold thong B over to the right and thong B1 to the left (Fig. 3). Bring thong A down over thong B and through the bight of thong B1; carry thong A1 up and over thong B1 and through the bight of thong B.

The braid in this second stage, before it is tightened, looks like the diagram in Fig. 4, and after it is tightened it is like that in Fig. 5.

In the previous move, the white and black thongs were worked clockwise, but in the third stage of this braid the reverse is true. The white and black thongs are both moved in a counter-clockwise direction.

Bring thong A downward and carry thong A1 upward. Pass thong B over thong A1 toward the left and through the bight of thong A; carry thong B1 to the right over thong A and through the bight of thong A1. This is indicated by the arrow-lines in Fig. 6, while the tightened braid is shown in Fig. 7. Continue in this fashion, first clockwise and then counter-clockwise.

To finish the braid, tuck the black thongs downward over the last bend and into the braid (Fig. 8), and do the same with the white ones. Or the braid may be finished with the terminal knot, as shown in Plate 15. In this braid the hair side of the leather is first on top and then on the under side. It is not too noticeable when the thongs are colored.

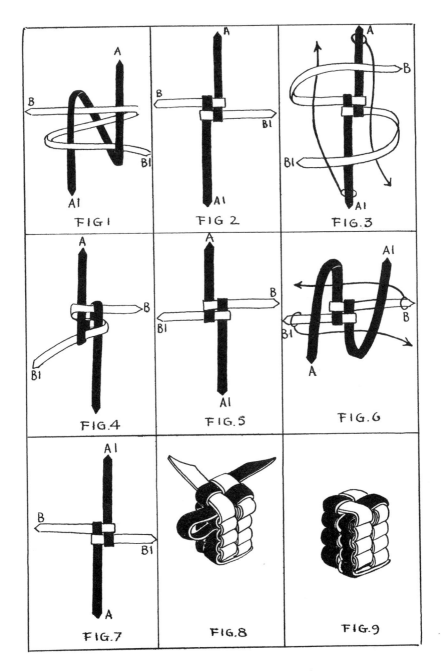

FIG 1 FIG 2 FIG.3

FIG.4 FIG.5 FIG.6

FIG.7 FIG.8 FIG.9

PLATE 22—Square Braid of Four Thongs.

45

PLATE 23

SPIRAL BRAID—This braid is also worked on the principle of super-imposed crown knots. While the previous braid gives a vertical effect in the pattern, this one gives a spiral effect.

It may be worked with six thongs, over a core, as will be shown later, but when four thongs are used, no heart or core is necessary.

The first step is the same as for the square braid in Plate 22. The result is shown in Fig. 1.

Take thong B1 and fold it over thong A1, indicated by the arrow-line in Fig. 1 and shown in Fig. 2. Next, fold thong A1 over thong B1 and thong B, as indicated by the arrow-line in Fig. 2 and shown in Fig. 3. Carry thong B over thong A1 and thong A, indicated and shown in Figs. 3 and 4, respectively.

In the last step of this stage, take thong A and pass it over thong B and through the bight of thong B1, indicated by the arrow-line in Fig. 4 and shown in Fig. 5.

The second phase, starting with Fig. 6 is executed in exactly the same fashion. Note the work moves continually in a counter-clockwise direction. However, if the start is clockwise, keep on working that way.

The completed braid is shown in Fig. 7.

SPIRAL TWIST BRAID—The spiral twist braid starts exactly as the spiral braid, shown in Fig. 1. In the next step, however, where B1 crosses to the right over A1, give the thong a half twist so that the smooth side remains uppermost (Fig. 8).

Bring thong A1 over thongs B1 and B and twist it so that the smooth side is up and the flesh side is in contact with the thongs beneath (Fig. 9).

The same twist is given each thong. Thus, when the braid is completed, the smooth side of the thong is exposed. In the diagram showing the finished braid (Fig. 12) the twists are emphasized; however, if it is worked carefully and each twist brought down close to the point where the thong emerges, the braid will present a finished appearance.

These braids may be used to make attractive and durable leashes, lanyards and bathrobe belts.

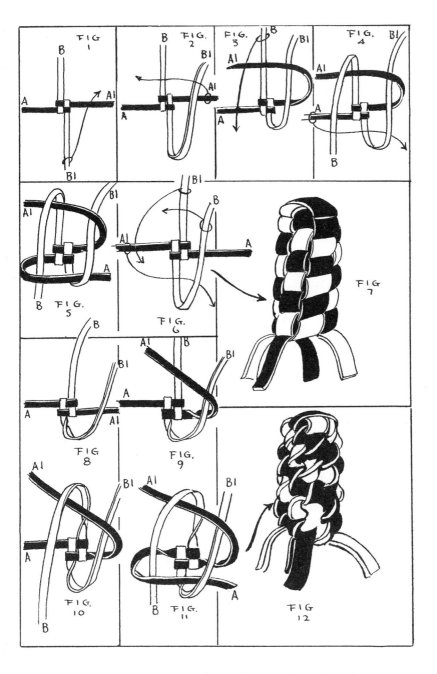

PLATE 23—Spiral Braid and Spiral Twist Braid.

47

PLATE 24

SQUARE BRAID OF EIGHT THONGS—While this beautiful braid is to all appearances a flat braid, after it is finished and moulded it becomes a square braid with four corners and four faces each showing exactly the same weave. It is of South American origin, where it is used mainly on bridles.

Cut a strip of leather into eight thongs of equal width, or lash together eight thongs. The entire procedure is the same as in flat braiding, but on the order of the thirteen and twenty-one thong double braids.

Group the thongs four on each side. Start with the right-hand thong, No. 8 in Fig. 1, and bring it to the left center under the three nearest thongs, 7, 6 and 5. Then bring the extreme left-hand thong, No. 1 to the right center over the three nearest thongs, 2, 3 and 4, and under thong 8. These steps are shown in Fig. 1.

Next bring thong 7 (on the extreme right) to the left center over the three nearest thongs, 6, 5 and 1. This is indicated by the arrow-line in Fig. 1 and shown in Fig. 2.

In the fourth step, bring thong 2 from the left to the right center, under the three nearest thongs, 3, 4 and 8 and over 7. This is indicated by the arrow-line in Fig. 2 and shown in Fig. 3.

Now thong 6 (on the extreme right) is brought to the left center under the three nearest thongs. This is the key to this braid.

Remember that the extreme right-hand thong alternates by going under three in one move and then over three thongs in the next; the extreme left-hand thong alternates by first going over three thongs and under one thong, then under three thongs and over one thong.

When the braid is of sufficient length, press on the edges to open them up, and in order to adjust the braid so it will be perfectly square, tap it lightly with a mallet on all four sides. This makes all sides the same width and of the same weave. (Fig. 7).

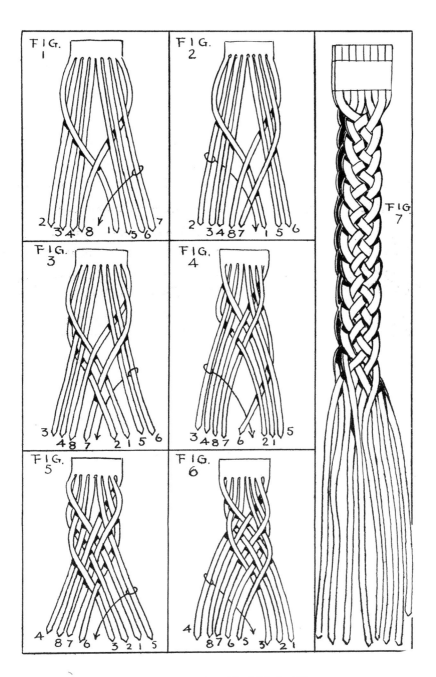

PLATE 24—Square Braid of Eight Thongs.

PLATE 25

Roll Button—This type of button is undoubtedly the most primitive of leather buttons. It is made very easily and is most practical. In South America the old-time gaucho used one of these buttons in place of a stirrup, hooking the button between his first two toes.

To make this simplest type of button, take a strip of leather, say one-half inch or three-quarters of an inch wide, taper it to a point and, about an inch and a half back from the point, make a horizontal slit as long as the leather is wide (Fig. 1). Dampen the leather, then turn the point inward and pull through (Fig. 2) and the button is complete. (Fig. 3).

I saw one of these buttons on the flap of a German Luger holster in World War II. It had seen much wear but was as serviceable as ever.

This type of button may be applied as a belt fastening as shown in Figs. 4, 5 and 6. It is passed through the slot while disengaged and then the button is formed when the tongue of the belt is in place. It can be used thus for all sorts of fastenings.

To make another type of roll button, taper a small strip of leather, wet it and then roll it up from the widest end (Fig. 7). When it is rolled about two-thirds of the way, cut a slot directly through the roll, pass the pointed end through (Fig. 8) and draw it tight (Fig. 9).

This button can be used on pocketbooks, boxes, etc., by leaving a long enough pointed end so that it can be fastened by the three-hole method as shown in Fig. 11.

A leather thong doubled and passed through four holes as shown in Fig. 10 serves as a fastener. To unloosen the button, pull on the pointed end.

The method of using this button as a clasp for a box is shown in Fig. 12. It is also good on leather hunting jackets, or wherever a button or clasp is needed.

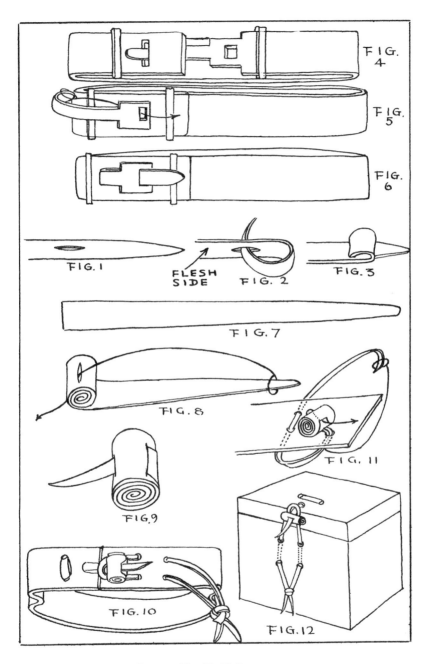

FIG. 4

FIG. 5

FIG. 6

FIG. 1

FLESH SIDE

FIG. 2

FIG. 3

FIG. 7

FIG. 8

FIG. 9

FIG. 11

FIG. 10

FIG. 12

PLATE 25—Roll Buttons.

51

PLATE 26

TWO-THONG TURK'S HEAD BUTTON—This is the same type of knot that is used by cowboys in tying the ends of their reins together. Made with a short thong of ⅛ inch in width, it is a practical button.

The first step is shown in Fig. 1 where the thong is doubled with the flesh sides together. Loop the end of thong B as shown and bring it around under A. Next, place A across the loop formed by B. Pass thong B over A and through this loop. (Fig. 2).

Bring thong A around underneath and up through its own loop as indicated by the arrow-line in Fig. 3. The loose knot is shown in Figs. 4 and 5. Tighten it by pulling easily on both ends of the thongs. See that the ends of the thongs have the flesh sides together.

The ends may be cut off flush with the knot or left to facilitate pulling the knot through the buttonhole.

THREE-THONG TURK'S HEAD BUTTON—This knot is made in the same manner as the Turk's Head terminal knot for round braid in Plate 15. In this case three thongs are used. Cut the leather with a tapered end. Split the larger end into three thongs, A, B, and C (Fig. 7).

Begin the crown knot as shown in Fig. 8 by folding the extreme right-hand thong, which is C, over thong B and behind thong A. Next, fold thong B over thong C and in front of thong A. Now fold thong A over thong B and in between thongs C and B at their base, as indicated in the arrow-line in Fig. 9.

Pass thong C around the base of thong A and up through the center. Then carry thong B around the base of thong C and up through the center. Pass thong A around the base of thong B and up through the center. These steps are indicated by the arrow-lines in Fig. 10. The finished knot is shown in Fig. 11.

To attach this button, cut three holes as shown in Fig. 12 and pass the end X down through the left-hand one, then up through the right-hand hole, down through the middle one and up through the left-hand hole, as indicated by the arrow-line in Fig. 12. This end also passes up through the center of the knot and forms one of the ends as shown by the arrow-line in Fig. 13. The ends may be trimmed or left, as desired. Attached in this manner, the button will remain firmly affixed indefinitely.

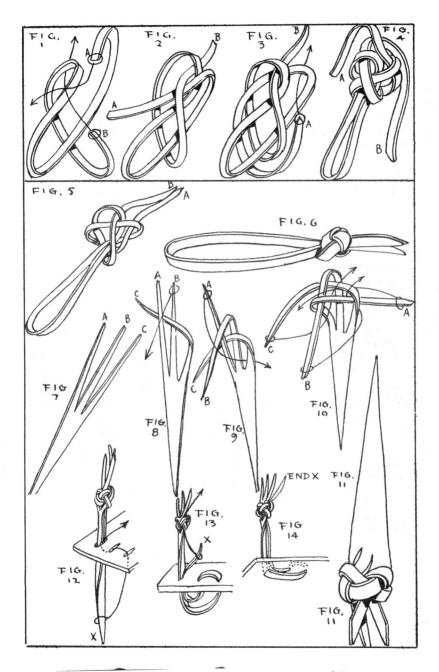

PLATE 26—Two and Three-Thong Turk's Head Button.

53

PLATE 27

CHINESE BUTTON KNOT—The basis of this knot is that which sailors term a Carrick Bend. Lay the thong over a mandrel as shown in Fig. 1, or around the hand. Twist thong B (on the right) into a loop as shown in Fig. 2 with the bight over thong A.

Bring thong A under thong B and in an over-one-under-one sequence, as indicated by the arrow-line in Fig. 2. Fig. 3 shows the completed Carrick Bend.

Bring the end of thong B up through the center on its own side as indicated by the arrow-line in Fig. 3. Thong A follows a similar course on its own side, as shown by the arrow-line.

Remove the loose knot from the mandrel, or the hand, and bring the two ends together, with their flesh sides touching. Begin to tighten the knot carefully, first taking up the bight which originally was around the mandrel. The knot now appears as shown in Fig. 4. Tighten it gradually, always holding the two ends together until finished, as shown in Fig. 5.

DIAMOND BUTTON KNOT—The diamond button knot starts in the same way as the Chinese button—with a Carrick Bend. The difference is in bringing up the ends through the center of the knot.

In the case of the Diamond Button Knot, instead of passing thong A up through the center on its own side, bring it around as indicated by the arrow-line in Fig. 6 and up on the side of thong B, passing under B. Carry thong B around to the side of thong A, pass it under thong A and up through the center.

The bight around the mandrel is the top of the button. Keep the flesh sides of the ends together and work out the slack until the knot becomes tight. This is a more attractive knot than the Chinese button knot.

Both can be made with a $\frac{1}{8}$ inch thong or wider one if desired.

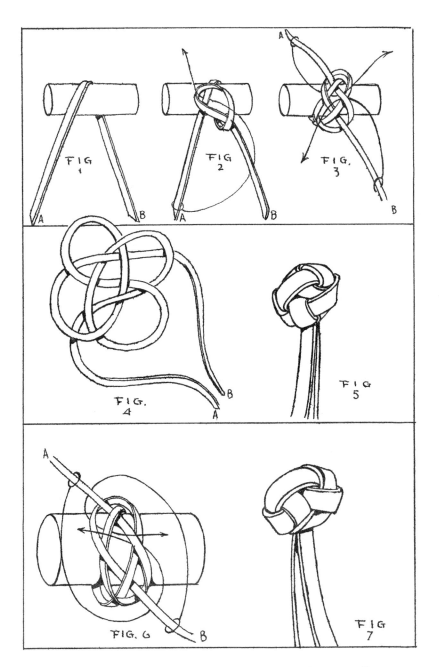

PLATE 27—Chinese Button Knot and Diamond Button Knot.

55

PLATE 28

Round Button of Four Thongs—To make this button take a piece of leather of ordinary thickness, 14 inches long and ¼ inch wide. Split in half 6 inches from each end, making four ⅛ inch thongs (Fig. 1).

Fold the leather with the flesh side in and make a crown knot as shown in Fig. 2. (This is made the same as shown in Fig. 1, Plate 22, under square braids.) Here the thongs are designated as A, B, C and D.

Next, with the thongs designated as A, B, C and D, make a wall knot, which is a crown knot done from underneath; in other words, pass thong A under thong B, thong B under thong C, thong C under thong D and thong D under or through the bight of thong A. See Fig. 3.

Draw up this wall knot so that it rests below the first, or crown knot. Now make another crown knot as shown in Fig. 4. This one is carefully worked down on top of the other two knots and appears as in Fig. 5.

The braiding or weaving process now begins. The sequence is over-two-under-two, as shown in Fig. 5, where the awl passes under two thongs to illustrate the course of thong C.

Pass thong C down over the two thongs below it and then up under two, the second of which is thong D. Then pass thong D down over the two below it and up under two, the upper one of which is thong A; thong A down over two and up under two, the top one being thong B; thong B downward over two and up under two, the upper one being thong C, which already has been tucked in place in the first move of this step.

The top of the knot now will appear as in Fig. 6. The thongs on top are in the form of a square. If an awl is inserted down in each corner it will go clear through the knot alongside the folded part of the leather. In Fig. 6 is shown the path of thong D. Working in a counter-clockwise direction, or to the left, arrow-lines indicate the paths of the other thongs. Pull them down through and cut them off underneath.

This button also can be made with three, six or eight thongs.

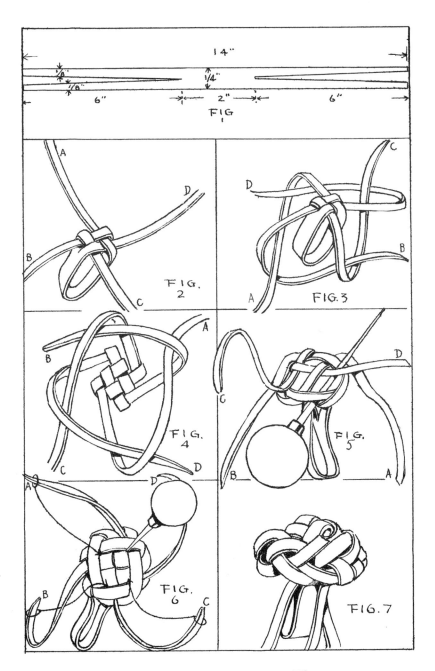

PLATE 28—Round Button of Four Thongs.

57

PLATE 29

SQUARE BUTTON OF FOUR THONGS—The square button of four thongs is started in the same way as the round button of four thongs described in Plate 28. Use the same length of leather, cut in the same fashion as indicated for the round button and shown again in Fig. 1.

Fold the leather at the uncut part with the flesh sides inward (Fig. 2). Make a crown knot as shown in Fig. 3, working the thongs toward the left or counter-clockwise. Tighten the knot as shown in Fig. 4.

The next knot, which is a wall knot, or crown knot made from beneath, is worked clockwise, or to the right, as shown in Fig. 5. This is important—the crown knot is worked to the *left* and the wall knot to the *right*.

The wall knot is drawn up snug just at the base of the crown knot.

The braiding or weaving of the knot is the next step. Start with thong D as shown in Fig. 7. Work this thong to the right and pass it back and down behind its own part as shown in Fig. 7. The same applies to the other three thongs. For instance, carry thong A to the right and down behind its own part; repeat likewise with thong B and thong C.

All the thongs now point downward.

The final step in making this button is illustrated in Fig. 8. Work the thongs toward the right and upward. Pass each around and over the one next to it and up through the knot, as shown and indicated by the arrow-line in Fig. 8. Thong B thus is brought over thong C and up through the knot. Thong C, in turn, passes over thong D and upward. And so on.

The ends may be cut flush with the top of the knot or pointed and left protruding.

This makes a very attractive button.

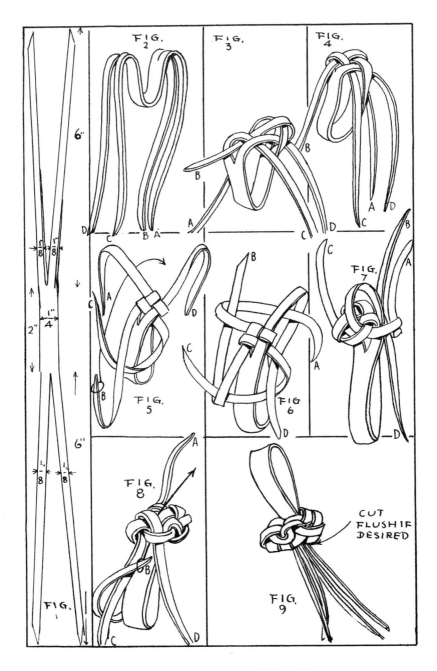

PLATE 29—Square Button of Four Thongs.

PLATE 30

SPANISH EDGE LACING OF ONE LOOP—Edge lacing serves two purposes. It joins the edges of two or more pieces of leather and provides a decorative finish to the work by covering the raw edges.

Use a lacing thong about four and one-half times the length of the edge to be covered.

Before making the holes or slits on the edges, it is best to thin down these edges with a skiving knife, tapering them on the flesh sides. Then carefully cement them together. In making the holes or slits take into consideration the width of the lacing to be used. A simple rule is that if a lacing of ⅛ inch is used, space the holes ⅛ inch apart and also ⅛ inch from the edge.

In the Spanish edge lacing, as well as in other types, it is more convenient to work from the left to the right. Run the lacing through the first left-hand hole from the front until only about ¼ inch of the end is left (Fig. 1).

Now insert the lacing back through the same hole, beneath the projecting end and draw tight (Figs. 2 and 3). The end is thus held fast. Before the loop is closed, apply a small amount of cement. Always work from the front.

Now carry the lacing through hole No. 2 (Fig. 3) and bring it around to the front again; this time it passes through its own loop (Fig. 4).

This loop and working part of the lacing always come together flesh side to flesh side. Tighten the first loop as shown in Fig. 5. Pass the lacing through hole No. 3, around to the front, through the loop, tighten the loop and proceed to the next hole. The finished lacing is shown in Figs. 7 and 8.

To insure even lacing always try to exert the same amount of pull each time. When finished, lay the work on a hard surface and gently tap the lacing down with a mallet. This distributes it and makes it lie flat.

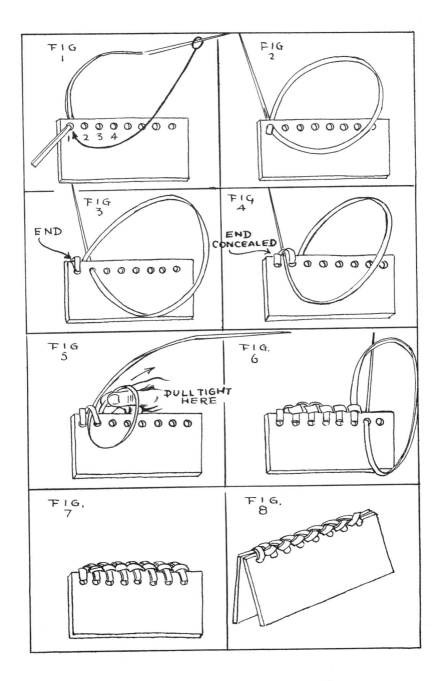

PLATE 30—Spanish Edge Lacing of One Loop.

PLATE 31

SPLICING—In edge lacing it is best to work with short lengths of lacing thongs and to splice on additional lengths as required. This will eliminate the trouble of continually pulling through a lengthy lacing, which not only is bothersome but also narrows down the lacing toward the working end.

In splicing, bevel both edges of the lacing (Fig. 1). Bevel the working lacing on the flesh side, the other on the smooth side. Thus the top edge of the spliced lacing passes through smoothly (Fig. 1). Touch with some quick-drying cement, either rubber or Duco, and press together. Be careful in using Duco for if it comes in contact with the finished side of the leather, it will eventually leave a light spot as the rest of the leather darkens.

JOINING—Sometimes the lacing will run entirely around, as on the edges of a bill-fold, and in such a case it can be joined together so that it will not be noticeable. In Fig. 2 the lacing on the right represents the start. It has gone completely around and has been brought up to the point indicated on the left. In beginning the lacing which has to be joined, do not fasten down the standing end A but leave a couple of inches free, as shown in Fig. 2.

Withdraw the end A entirely from hole No. 2 and insert end B only through the first piece of leather, allowing it to come up between the two layers as shown in Fig. 3.

Take end A and bring it from the rear forward through the loop of end B and then from the front to the rear through its own loop (Fig. 4). The next step, not shown in the sketch, is to bring end A from the rear forward through hole 2 but, only through the one layer of leather and up alongside end B. Tighten the braid, touch a little cement between the two ends, down as far as possible, cut them off and tuck them in. It will be impossible to see where this lacing has been joined.

To end a lacing that is not to be joined, follow the procedure illustrated in Figs. 6 and 7. This will provide a knot which will hold fast.

In going around corners with any type of edge lacing, always pass through the corner hole two or three times to space the lacing on the outer edge as shown in Fig. 8.

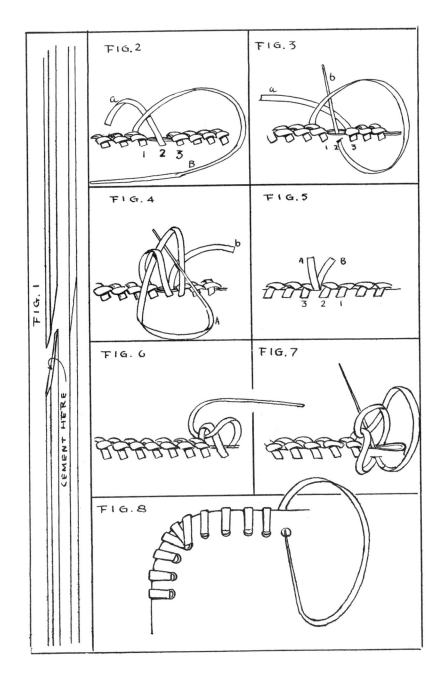

FIG. 1

CEMENT HERE

FIG. 2

FIG. 3

FIG. 4

FIG. 5

FIG. 6

FIG. 7

FIG. 8

PLATE 31—Splicing and Joining Edge Lacing.

PLATE 32

SPANISH EDGE LACING OF TWO LOOPS—Use a thong about six times the length of the edge to be covered.

Start with the standing end in the back, held down by the thumb between the first and second hole. Then pass the thong from the front to the rear through hole No. 1 as shown in Fig. 1. Bring the thong forward again and pass it through hole No. 2 from front to rear, also shown in Fig. 1.

Bring the thong to the front again, and this time, instead of passing it through a hole, carry it beneath the two loops formed on the top as shown in Fig. 2. Tighten the work by pulling at the two points indicated in Fig. 3. Always try to exert the same tension so that the lacing will be consistently even.

After passing the thong under the two loops, bring it to the front again and this time pass it through hole No. 3 as shown in Fig. 4. Bring it to the front and pass it under the two loops as shown in Fig. 5. Tighten by pulling upon that portion of the thong indicated in Fig. 5.

The sequence now is through hole No. 4 from front to back and then under the two loops on the top; tighten (Fig. 6); then through hole No. 5 and under the two loops; and so on.

JOINING SPANISH EDGE LACING OF TWO LOOPS—Where the edge lacing goes completely around as on a wallet or bill-fold and comes back to the starting point, finish the work by joining the braid. When this is done properly it is difficult to tell where the braid ends or begins.

Note in Fig. 7 at the starting point the standing end is shown in dotted lines. The standing end is withdrawn through the starting hole and the loops through which it had passed. It is shown protruding from hole No. 2 in Fig. 8.

The braid has come completely around and the working end is shown in Fig. 9 just to the left of the starting hole. Pass it through this hole from the front, up through the loop to the right, and under the intersection of the two loops to the left, as indicated by the arrow-line in Fig. 10. Then pass it back over its own part, down through the right-hand loop and into the same hole in which is the standing end (Fig. 11).

When binding together two pieces of leather tuck both ends inside between the two pieces and the braid is complete.

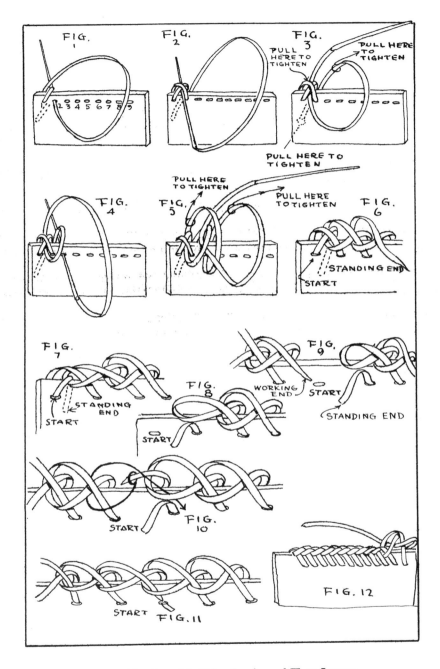

PLATE 32—Spanish Edge Lacing of Two Loops.

65

PLATE 33

SPANISH EDGE LACING OF THREE LOOPS—For this edge lacing, use a thonging lace about seven and one-half times the length to be worked. Start by passing the thong from the front to the rear through hole 2 and folding the end over the edge to the back between holes 1 and 2. This end is shown in dotted lines in Fig. 1.

Next, bring the working end to the front and pass it through hole 1 and to the front again and through hole 3. Do not draw the loops tight.

There are three of these loops on the edge of the leather. Now pass the working end through the three loops from the front to the rear (Fig. 2), bring it forward and pass it through hole 4 from the front (Fig. 3).

Tighten the start of the braid by drawing on it in the same sequence it was made and in the same direction, but leave the last three loops slightly loose so the working end can pass through them easily. The original end, shown in dotted lines, should be secured beneath one of its own parts.

In Fig. 4 the working end is shown passing through the second set of three loops. Bring it to the front and then down through hole 5. Continue the braid in this way until the finish, when it is tapped lightly with a hammer or mallet to make it lie smoothly.

TWO-TONE SPANISH EDGE LACING OF ONE LOOP—If a two-tone effect on edge lacing is desired, use two thongs of different colors. In the illustration we will designate thong A as white and thong B as black. Always work from the front to the rear. First introduce thong A through hole 1 and then thong B through hole 2. Bring thong A to the front and through hole 3 (Fig. 6).

Now pass thong B through the loop of thong A from the front to the rear and to the left of its own part, as shown in Fig. 7. Bring it forward and through hole 4, as shown. Pass thong A through the loop of thong B and to the left of its own part, and bring it forward and through hole 5 (Fig. 8). Continue thus until the end, first working with one thong and then the other. The standing ends at the beginning can be folded over and secured in the rear beneath their own parts.

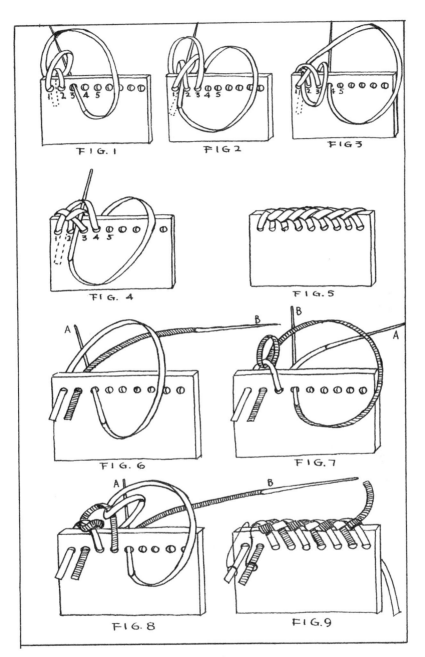

PLATE 33—Top: Spanish Edge Lacing of Three Loops.
Bottom: Two-Tone Spanish Edge Lacing of One Loop.

PLATE 34

Round Braid Edge Lacing—This edge lacing resembles the four-thong round braid, except that it is made with one thong. There are several methods of making this beautiful edge lacing. Here we will consider the first:

Start with a thong at least seven times the length of the edge to be covered. Space the holes the same as the width of the lacing and punch them this same distance from the edge.

Pass the thong through hole 1 from the front; forward and through hole 3 from the front; the same through hole 5 (Fig. 1); then 7 and finally 9. If the edge lacing is longer, keep on passing the thong to the right through every other hole. Leave an extra hole (Hole No. 10) at the end as shown (Fig. 2).

Now to start working back. From hole 9 go back through 7 as indicated by the arrow-line in Fig. 2. Continue back toward the starting point until hole 2 is reached. Pass the end through hole 2, as indicated by the arrow-line in Fig. 3.

In the next step, work towards the right, passing the thong through holes 4, 6, 8 and 10 (Figs. 4 and 5).

Now the actual braid begins. The working end of the thong is in the rear of hole 10. Bring it forward over its own part and under the next thong.

This step is indicated by the fid in Fig. 6. The thong follows the same course. Carry it through hole 8 (Fig. 7), and in the rear pass it under the thong to the left of it, as can be seen in Fig. 8, then over the next and under the next (Fig. 8). The awl is shown passing through hole 6 in Fig. 8, which will be the course of the thong. On the other side, pass it under one, then over one on top and under one in the front. Continue until it joins the standing end which is in hole 1.

This braid lies flat and entirely covers the raw edge of the leather. It has many uses on saddles, pistol holsters, knife sheaths, etc.

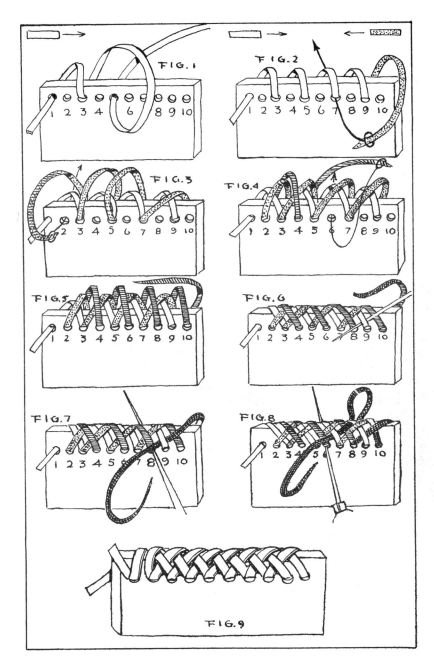

PLATE 34—Round Braid Edge Lacing.

PLATE 35

Round Braid Edge Lacing (Second Method)—Here is another way to make the four-part round braid edge lacing of one thong. Start as in Fig. 1 by passing the thong through hole 1 from rear to front; then over the edge to the rear and forward through hole 4.

In the next step, also shown in Fig. 1, bring the working end to the left and forward through hole 2 from the rear to the front.

In Fig. 2 the working end is shown passing over the edge and through hole 5 from rear to front. Up to this point the working end of the thong has been passed over its own parts. However, in Fig. 2 the arrow-line indicates how the working end in the next move passes to the rear over its own part and beneath the loop of that part of the thong over hole 4.

Bring the working end of the thong forward through hole 3 as shown in Fig. 3. The fid, with its end beneath the thong which emerges from hole 4, also shown in Fig. 3.

After passing the working end beneath the thong at hole 4, carry it over the edge, to the rear, and forward through hole 6 (Fig. 4). Pass it over its own part and under that part of the thong illustrated by the course of the fid in Fig. 4.

Next, bring the working end from the rear to the front through hole 4, which is already occupied by a section of the thong (Fig. 5). Pass it beneath the section of the thong which emerges from hole 5, as shown by the fid in Fig. 5. Now move the working end to the rear and forward through hole 7. Pass it over its own part and under a section of the thong as in Fig. 4, and then through hole 5 to the front—and so on until the finish. The sequence is always over-one-under-one. If the original standing end has been left long it can be worked forward to close up the braid at the beginning, following the over-one-under-one sequence.

Round Braid Edge Lacing (Third Method)—By using four thongs, all of different colors, or two of one color and two of another, you can obtain a multi-tone braid as shown in the sequences in Figs. 7, 8, 9, 10, 11 and 12.

Work with two thongs at a time, lacing the first pair from left to right to the end and then interweaving the next pair. Remember the over-one-under-one-sequence.

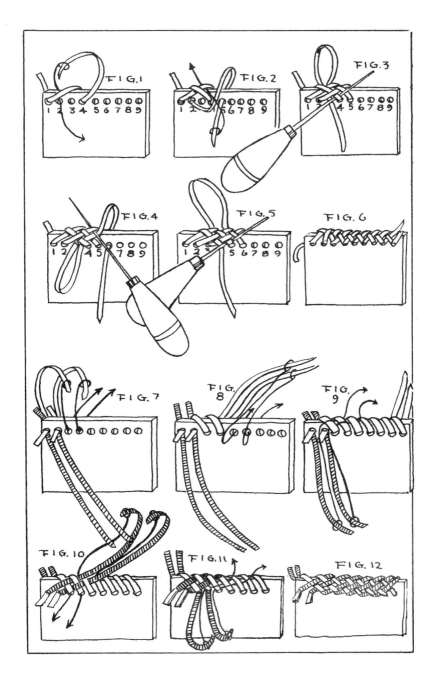

PLATE 35—Round Braid Edge Lacing.

71

PLATE 36

Use of Spanish Edge Lacing in Attaching Pockets and Flaps
—First, cut out the pocket patch marked A in Fig. 1. Around the three edges to be laced on, punch holes about ⅛ inch from the edge and about 3/16 of an inch apart. Lay the pocket patch on the part to which it will be fastened and insert a fid or other pointed instrument into each hole, making a corresponding impression on the leather foundation, marked B.

Punch out these holes at the impressions on B. About ¼ inch from this row of holes, punch the same number of holes in the leather B, each opposite a hole in the inner row. At the curves of the pockets these holes will be spaced wider apart than those on the inner circle—but there should be an equal number of holes on both inner and outer circles.

With a little cement around the edge of the under part, affix the pocket flap, being careful that the holes in the flap are directly over those on the leather beneath. Turn back the flap at the upper right-hand corner and pass the thong (3/32 inch commercial lacing is best) through the first inner hole in the leather B and back up through the outer hole (Fig. 1). Lay the flap corner back with a little more cement on it and on the end of the lacing so that the latter is held fast, and pass the needle through the hole in flap A and down through the corresponding hole in the leather B (the same through which the lacing was first inserted) and up through the second outer hole in B (Fig. 2).

Bring the working end (shown with needle attached) down through the loop formed by the lacing, keeping it inclined to the right (Fig. 3). Draw it snug. Pass the needle down through the second inner hole and up through the outer third hole (Fig. 4). Next, bring it down through the loop formed between the second set of holes (Fig. 5). Pass it down through the inner hole, No. 3, and up through the outer hole, No. 4, and again down through the loop formed. It will be seen by now that this is the same as the Spanish edge lacing of one loop (Plate 30).

Staggered Slits—To make the thong lie snug on the edge, slant and stagger the slits as shown on the pistol holster in Fig. 7.

Miscellaneous Edge Lacings—Fig. 8 shows a one-thong spiral or whip-lace; Fig. 9, double one-thong spiral; Fig. 10, double two-thong spiral; Fig. 11, two-thong plain spiral; Fig. 12, one-thong alternate spiral; Fig. 13, two-thong alternate spiral; Fig. 14, one-thong novelty spiral; Fig. 15, a Venetian spiral. The latter is made with very wide, thin lacing.

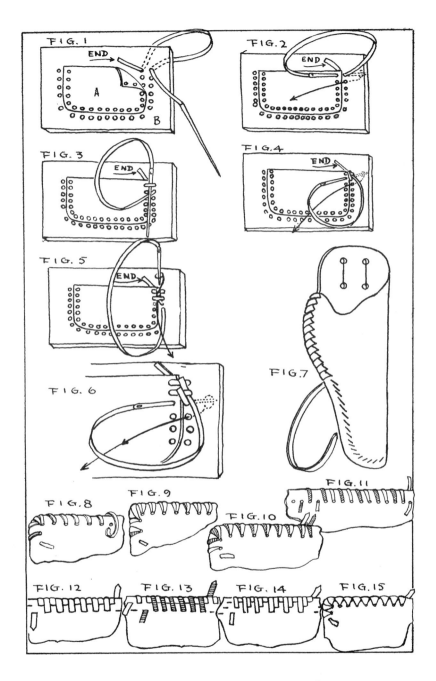

PLATE 36—Applications of Edge Lacing.

PLATE 37

Spanish Type Buckle Covering of One Loop—This is similar to the Spanish edge lacing of one loop and, once started, is worked in the same fashion (Plate 30).

In the standing end of the thong or lacing cut a small slit and widen it with the fid. Hold the buckle in the left hand with the front toward you. Place the lacing as shown in Fig. 1. Pass the working end, or pointed end, of the lacing through the slit as indicated by the arrow-line in Fig. 1 and draw the loop tight. If the tongue of the buckle is free to slide back and forth on the heel of the buckle, be sure it is held in the center.

Pass the lacing beneath the metal part of the buckle from the front, leaving a bight as shown in Fig. 2. The arrow-line in Fig. 2 indicates the path of the lacing in the next step. It enters from the front.

Pull out the slack as shown in Fig. 3, but leave a small bight or loop at the pulling point. The lacing again passes beneath the metal part of the buckle and to the rear.

Bring the lacing to the front over the metal part of the buckle. Under the bight which was left, place the fid (Fig. 4) and insert the point of the lacing through this part. Tighten as shown in Fig. 5. Next, pass the lacing beneath the metal part from the front as shown in Fig. 6. Bring it forward over the buckle and through the bight as indicated by the fid in Fig. 7.

Continue thus around the metal part of the buckle. The sequence is always the same: The lacing passes from the front to the rear beneath the metal and then goes through the resulting loop, also passing from front to rear.

Be careful to keep the braid on the outer edge of the buckle. Work it rather tightly so that it holds, but keep the tension consistent.

After working around the buckle and the braid is on the left-hand side of the buckle tongue, draw tight and cement the end to the leather itself. The start and finish of the braid will be hidden when the buckle is attached to the belt.

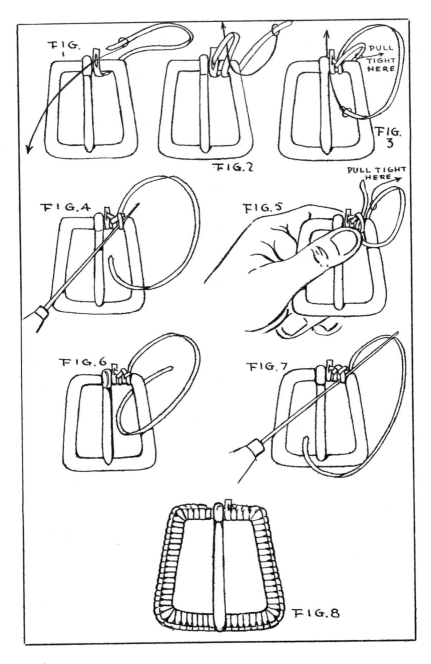

PLATE 37—Spanish Type Buckle Covering of One Loop.

PLATE 38

SPANISH TYPE BUCKLE COVERING OF TWO LOOPS—This is similar to the Spanish edge lacing of two loops (Plate 32) but is worked backwards.

Slit the standing end of the leather thong or lacing and place this end on the left side of the buckle as shown in Fig. 1. Pass the point of the lacing through the slit and bring it to the front. Tighten and pass the lacing beneath the metal part of the buckle and between the original loop and the tongue, that is, to the right of the original loop and left of the tongue (Fig. 2).

Bring the lacing to the front, over the buckle and over the original loop as shown in Fig. 3. Tighten and push the lacing against the tongue of the buckle, being sure the tongue is in the center.

Again, pass the lacing under the metal part as shown in Fig. 3. Insert the fid between this last loop and the original loop and under two loops of the lacing. This step is clearly illustrated in Fig. 3. The lacing follows the course of the fid; again, bring the lacing to the front and under the metal part (Fig. 4).

The fid makes an opening under the two loops as shown in Fig. 5. Be sure that the working end of the lacing always comes out in the rear to the right of its own loop. This is shown in Fig. 6.

Follow this sequence around the metal part of the buckle until the right-hand side is reached. Each time bring the lacing over to the front and under the metal part and then again to the front and under two loops.

This braid must be fairly snug on the metal so that it will not slip. Don't worry about the corners. The underneath loops may overlap slightly but the braid on top will be even.

By thus working this braid backwards it can be kept tight at all times. However, it can be worked as in the edge lacing of two loops, that is, from left to right.

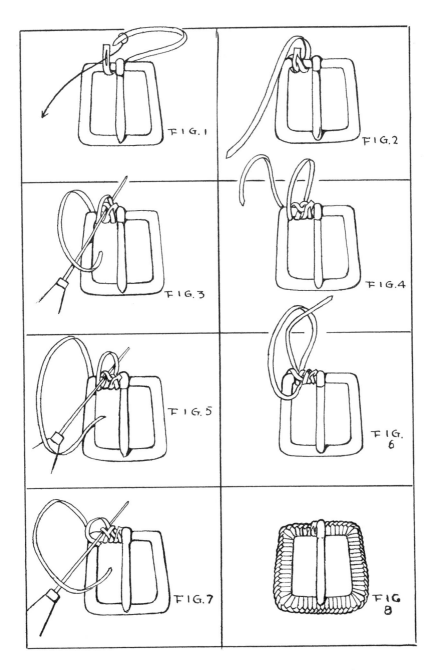

PLATE 38—Spanish Type Buckle Covering of Two Loops.

PLATE 39

SPANISH TYPE BUCKLE COVERING OF THREE LOOPS—This is similar to the Spanish edge lacing of three loops, except that it is worked backwards.

Hold the buckle with the front toward you and place the thong as shown in Fig. 1. If the tongue or pin of the buckle is movable, be sure that it is in the center before the braiding is started.

Pass the working end through the buckle, inclining it toward the tongue and to the right of the standing part as in Fig. 2.

Pass it through a second time, also inclining it to the right of both loops now around the metal heel of the buckle, as indicated by the arrow-line in Fig. 2 and shown in Fig. 3.

Bring it down and forward and pass it through the buckle the third time, now inclining it toward the left, as indicated in Fig. 3 and shown in Fig. 4.

It is sometimes difficult to get started, as the loops must not be too tight. At this stage compare your beginning with Fig. 4 to be sure all the loops are in the right place.

The next step has been illustrated in three different ways. First, in Fig. 4, it is shown by the arrow-line. Next, in Fig. 5, it has been shown by inserting the fid in the portion through which the thong passes. In Fig 6, the thong has passed through this place, under three other thongs and emerged on the top.

The thong does not, in this instance, pass around the metal part of the buckle. It comes down in front, inclines to the right and passes beneath the three thongs.

In the next step, which is the beginning of the second stage of the braid, bring the thong down to the front, pass it through the buckle and around the metal part, indicated by the arrow-line in Fig. 6 and shown in Fig. 7.

Again the fid is inserted beneath two thongs and under the loop, which makes three thongs (Fig. 7).

Pass the working part of the thong back to the front, over the metal part of the buckle, then down toward the right and through the course followed by the fid, under the three thongs, and, as before, over the metal part.

Continue this until the lacing is completely around the buckle and on the side of the tongue opposite to the starting point. This braid will make a thing of beauty of an ordinary buckle.

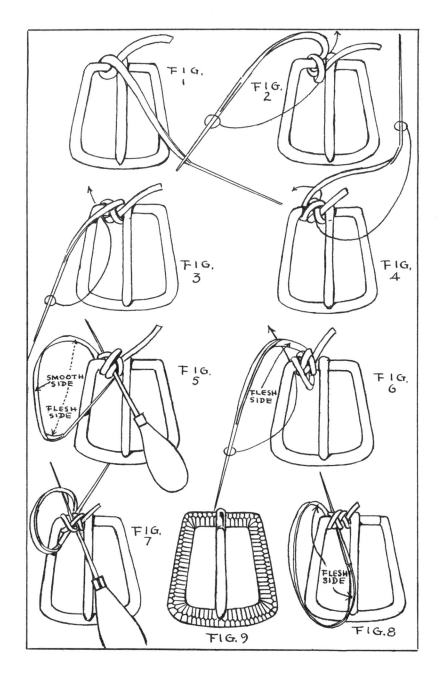

PLATE 39—Spanish Type Buckle Covering of Three Loops.

PLATE 40

SLIT LEATHER HANDLE COVERING OF ONE THONG—Cut a piece of leather the length of the handle to be covered. The supposed handle is shown in Fig. 2 and the corresponding piece of leather in Fig. 1. Then wrap the leather around the handle and cut off so that the ends exactly meet.

Now slit the leather so that it is divided into five sections, A, B, C, D, and E, (Fig. 1). The leather may be slit into more or less than five sections if desired so long as the total is an uneven number; for example: three or seven sections.

The thong (Fig. 3) should be the same width as the width of each section.

Lash the leather around the top of the core as shown in Fig. 4. Insert the end of the thong under the right-hand edge of the leather with some cement on both sides so that it will hold to both the leather and the handle. It is better to thin this part so it will not bulge through the leather.

Bring the thong to the left over the first section, which is E, Fig. 4; then under the next, which is section D (Fig. 5); over the next (not shown in the diagram, but which is section C); under B, over A and under E (Fig. 6). Continue this alternative weave of over one, under one.

Keep working the thong up snug but also keep the leather pulled down. Go around and around until the thong will pass through the last slit without pinching the leather. Conceal the working end inside the leather covering and lash down the bottom.

This gives a vertical pattern and is very effective with contrasting leather and thong (Fig. 7).

To obtain a spiral pattern, cut the leather covering as explained above. This example shows six slits, dividing the leather into seven sections (Fig. 8). The thong should be one-half the width of each section. Start as before but go over two sections (Fig. 9), then under two sections, and then over two (Fig. 10).

Keep up this sequence of over two, under two, until the bottom is reached. The effect is shown in Fig. 11.

The bottom and top of this covering may be concealed with Turk's Heads or woven knots, as explained later in the book under Turk's Heads and Spanish Knots, beginning with Plate 46.

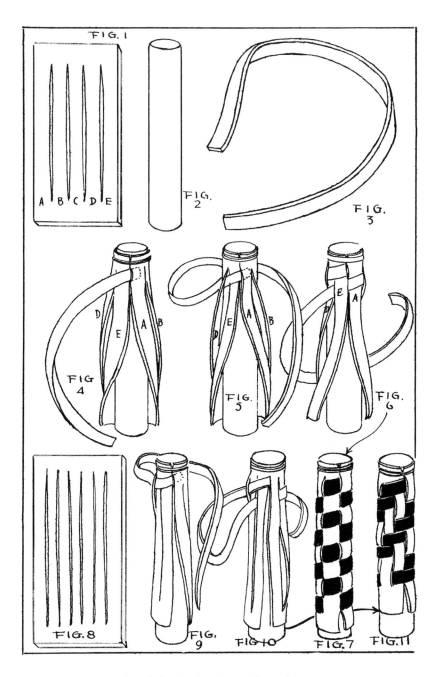

PLATE 40—Slit Leather Covering of One Thong.

81

PLATE 41

SPANISH HITCHING—For the sake of clarity in the illustration a minimum of thongs has been used and larger spaces left between them than is actually necessary in the working of this braid.

Space the thongs around the circumference of the handle so that a space is left between each one equal to the width of the thong; that is, if ⅛ inch thongs are used, leave a space between them of ⅛ inch.

Take a longer thong, which is designated as thong X in Fig. 1. Slit one end and fasten it around the top, thus binding on the other thongs as shown in Fig. 1.

Pass the thong X around the core in a counter-clockwise direction. Bring thong No. 2 over thong X and then under to the left of its own part, as shown in Fig. 2. Thong No. 3 is brought over and then under and to its left. Repeat this operation with thongs 4 and 1.

On each turn of the longer thong, tighten up the braid by pulling the other thongs, and keep the work snug. As in all braiding, a consistent pull must be used to keep the braid even.

Continuation of the work is shown in Fig. 3 and in Fig. 4 is a clearer key to the braiding process. When the handle is completely covered, lash down the working ends of the thongs. Both top and bottom will be covered with Turk's Heads or Spanish knots, detailed later. The finished braid is shown in Fig. 5.

ZIG-ZAG BRAID—This braid is worked in the opposite way from the above braid but on the same principle. First, wrap the longer thong around the handle from top to bottom in a spiral fashion. It should not be too tight and it is well to saddle-soap the thong thoroughly before winding it around the core.

Work down with one thong at a time as shown in Fig. 6. The pattern can be varied by working the hitch either to the right or to the left. Use different colored thongs if desired.

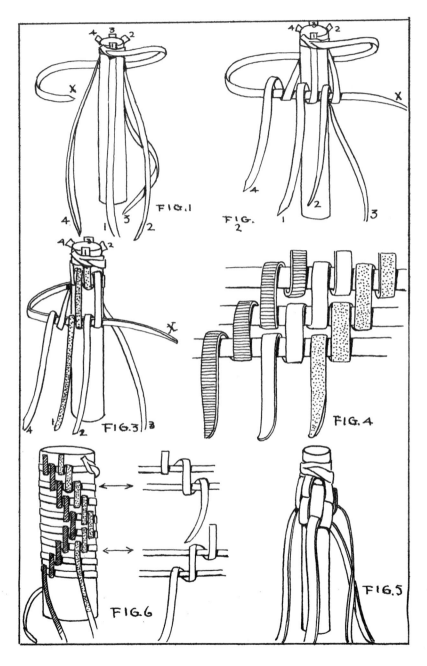

PLATE 41—Spanish Hitching and Zig-Zag Braid.

PLATE 42

Mosaic Type Braid—This is similar to the slit leather covering with one thong shown in Plate 40, but it is worked with independent thongs, which will enable one to vary the color of the thongs to form various chromatic patterns.

In the illustrations spaces have been left between the thongs which are lashed to the core. In the actual work, however, these should be close together. Thus, if the circumference is one and one-eighth inches, nine $\frac{1}{8}$ inch thongs will be needed. An uneven number is always required.

The longer thong, which is wound around the core, should be the same width as those lashed to the core. Slit it, pass the end through and tighten it over and around the other thongs as in Fig. 1.

Working counter-clockwise, pass the long thong under thong 1 and over thong 2; then under and over all the way around. When back to thong 1, pass the long thong over, and at thong 2 pass it under.

A spiral effect may be obtained by passing under two thongs and over two thongs.

Horizontal Braid—This is similar to Spanish hitching except that it is worked horizontally. The thongs, in this case thirteen, are lashed about the core, and the long thong is tightened at the top of the handle. Pass the long thong beneath thongs 4 and 3, bring it back around thong 3 and then under 3 and 2 (Fig. 4).

This is the sequence: Under two, over one, under two, over one. When back to the starting point it will be noticed that the long thong passes under 4 and 3, over 3 and under 3 and 2. The arrow-line indicates the next step.

Fig. 6 is an enlargement of the way the braid is worked. In Fig. 7, it is shown how, instead of going under two and over one, you pass over two and under one.

Hitching—This is done entirely with one thong. Pass the thong around the core and over its own end as in Fig. 8, before the hitching begins. Pass the thong over the part around the core, behind it, and then over its own part. In the illustrations this braid appears loose, but in the actual working it should be kept tight.

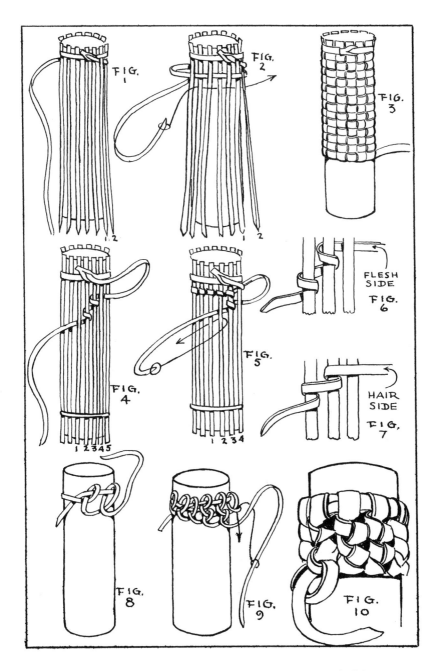

PLATE 42—Mosaic Type—Horizontal Braid—Hitching.

PLATE 43

Four-Thong Twist Braid Covering—This, as well as similar braids shown in Plates 22 and 23, can be used for handle covering. When working with a core, or heart, usually six thongs are employed, but for the purpose of simplifying the technique, four thongs are used in the illustration.

The sum of the width of the thongs should equal the circumference of the handle to be covered. That is, if the handle measures one inch around, each thong should be $\frac{1}{4}$ inch.

Lash the thongs, flesh sides out, to the bottom of the handle, as shown in Fig. 1. The first step is the same as in the square braid in Plate 22. Bring thong 1 up inclined to the right (Fig. 2). The smooth or hair side is now uppermost. The arrow-line in Fig. 2 indicates the course of thong 2.

Bring thong 2 up under and then over thong 1 (Fig. 3). Bring thong 3 up and over thong 2 in the same fashion, as indicated by the arrow-line in Fig. 3.

In the next step, bring thong 4 up and over thong 3 and then pass it through the bight or loop of thong 1. This is indicated by the arrow-line in Fig. 4 and shown in Fig. 5. Work the braid down snug, in fact rather tightly, as shown in Fig. 6, which view is straight down on the braid from the top.

Continue now in the same direction, or counter-clockwise, and pass each thong over the one to its right: 1 over 2; 2 over 3, and so on. When thong 4 is reached and has been brought over thong 3 it goes down through the bight or loop of thong 1.

However, as shown in Fig. 7, each thong is twisted or given a half turn at its base so the smooth side always is uppermost. Care should be taken that this twist is as close as possible to the base, and as each section is tightened be sure that the smooth side is out. This is the purpose of the twist. In some cases it will be necessary to use your fid in readjusting this twist after tightening.

The colors of the thongs may be varied. When the twists have all been evened up, roll and braid gently under your foot to smooth it out.

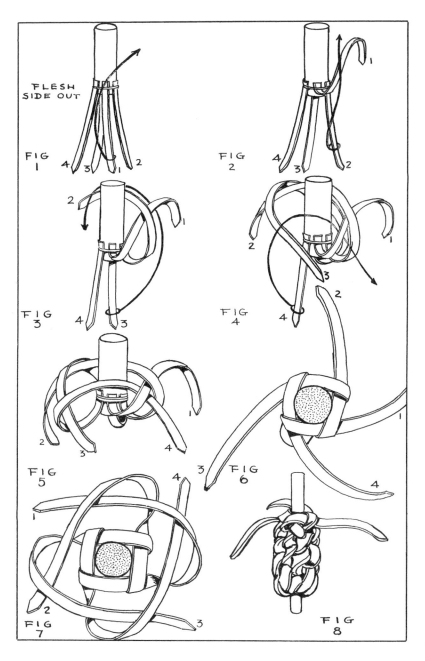

FLESH SIDE OUT

FIG 1

FIG 2

FIG 3

FIG 4

FIG 5

FIG 6

FIG 7

FIG 8

PLATE 43—Four-Thong Twist Braid Covering.

87

PLATE 44

SIX-THONG MULTIPLE BRAID—In this type of braid both ends are finished and need not be covered. It is popular in covering a core with varied circumferences as the process of first spiraling the thongs makes it possible to compensate for bulges and depressions. Six thongs are used. Their total width should be the same as the circumference of the core, although this is not absolutely necessary.

Lash the thongs to the bottom of the core, as shown in Fig. 1, with the flesh sides out. Bring thong 1 up and over the lashing and spiral it around the core as shown in Fig. 2; then thong 2, keeping it snugly along the under side of 1 (Fig. 3).

Continue to spiral the other thongs, smooth side out, until they are all at the top and close together as shown in Fig. 4. Lash them at the top in this position.

A crown knot is formed with the six thongs as shown in Fig. 5. For instance, thong 1 is turned downward, behind 2, smooth side out. Pass thong 6 beneath thong 1; 5 beneath 6; 4 beneath 5; 3 beneath 4; and 2 beneath 3.

Begin the over and under sequence, braiding downward at a corresponding angle of the spiral thongs. Pass over one, under one (Fig. 6), or over two under two (Fig. 7). In fact it can be varied in the over and under sequence to suit, being sure that where one thong goes over two and under two the other five also go over two and under two. In this case the sequence is varied so that it is first under one, over one and then over two, under two (Fig. 7). The bottom is finished off in the over-one-under-one sequence (Fig. 8). Tuck the ends out of sight.

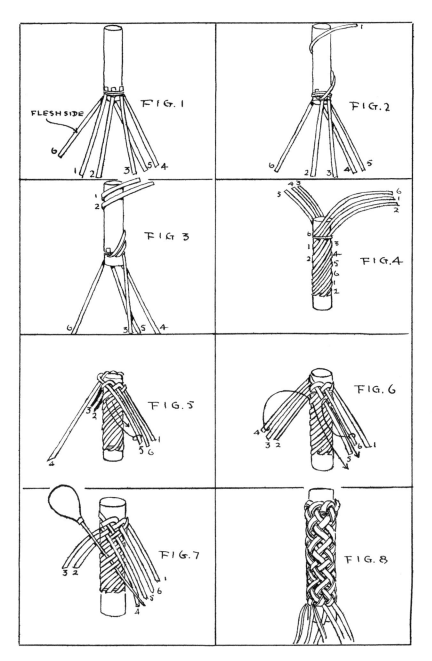

PLATE 44—Six-Thong Multiple Braid.

PLATE 45

MULTIPLE BRAID TOP AND CORE COVERING—This braid may be used to cover the top of any handle as well as the handle itself. Here is shown the over-one-under-one sequence, but it can be developed into over-two-under-two or other combinations of braids. Start by arranging the thongs in the sequence desired to cover the quirt handle, cane or other similar object.

In Fig. 1 the thongs are laid out in the manner shown. The core to be covered is illustrated just beneath, in Fig. 2. After weaving the thongs in their middle on a flat surface, push them close together and then lay this braided part on the top of the core, which should be slightly rounded at the top (Fig. 3). Secure the thongs just below the braid with cord or thread, as shown in Fig. 4, and arrange them evenly at the top.

In this braid, like any others around a core, the total width of the thongs should be equal to the circumference of the core. In this braid sixteen thongs are used. The measurement around the core is two inches, therefore, each thong is ⅛ inch wide.

Take every other thong (as in Fig. 5 even numbers have been taken) and pass each upward. It is best, as shown in Fig. 6, to tie these together with a string, so that they will be out of the way for the time being. It will be noticed that the thongs carried upward are those which come from beneath other thongs.

The thongs with uneven numbers are spiraled around the core to the full length (Fig. 6). Tie them at the bottom and be sure they are not too tight, but are edge to edge. This may not be possible at the very top, but in any event get them as close together as possible without disarranging the braid.

Take one of the upper thongs, in this case No. 12, and after having made a path for it with the fid (Fig. 7), braid it over the first one to its right, No. 11, and under the next one, which is No. 9. Then take thong 14 (Fig. 8) and braid it in a similar manner, over the first one to its right, which is thong 13, and under the next one, which is thong 11. Continue around, braiding each of the upper thongs over one and under one. Then start back with thong 12 and braid it over one and under one, and so on until the bottom is reached.

Incline these thongs in the upper group at an angle to the right, corresponding to the angle to the left of those which are spiraled around the core. Work the braid up carefully, tightening the thongs until they are snug. Remove the upper binding.

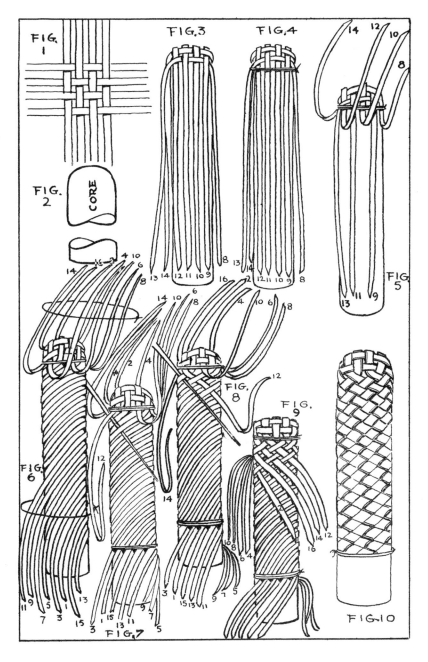

FIG. 1

FIG. 2

CORE

FIG. 3

FIG. 4

FIG. 5

FIG. 6

FIG. 7

FIG. 8

FIG. 9

FIG. 10

PLATE 45—Multiple Braid Top and Core Covering.

91

PLATE 46

BRAIDED PAPER TURK'S HEAD—The so-called Turk's Head, while serving a practical purpose in leather braiding, should be considered more as the basis or foundation for the beautiful Spanish woven knots.

The Turk's Head has long been one of the most puzzling of knots for the amateur. Observing the finished knot, it seems almost impossible to follow the course of the thong.

Basically the Turk's Head is simple. It is in every respect symmetrical completely around its circumference, and, like the flat braid, is amphichiral, that is, having the right and left sides alike in figure or pattern and dimensions. It presents the same appearance at any point and in the true Turk's Head the working end of the thong always comes back to the exact starting point, or the same place as the standing end, when the knot is complete.

The Turk's Head might be defined as an endless ring or wreath of any one of the flat braids. To demonstrate the anatomy of a Turk's Head the simplest of the flat braids has been used, the so-called hair braid of three thongs (Plate 4).

Take a strip of writing paper of the size shown in Fig. 1. Cut it into three smaller strips, leaving the section at the top closed, as shown by the dotted lines in Fig. 1.

Now braid these three strips into a three-part hair braid. In doing this, remember the law governing Turk's Heads. No Turk's Head may have the same number of bights, or outer loops (Fig. 2), as it has number of thongs across, or as they are termed parts. Nor can a Turk's Head have a number of bights and a number of parts which have a common divisor.

For example this Turk's Head is composed of three parts. Therefore, it cannot have three bights, nor six, nine, twelve, nor any number divisible by three. This law applies to all Turk's Heads.

An example with four bights: When the ends are pasted to the uncut portion of the paper as shown in Fig. 4 this immediate part forms one bight. The other three are plainly shown. After pasting down the ends, cut the closed portion, and the Turk's Head reveals itself as an endless wreath of three parts and four bights (Fig. 5).

To demonstrate, place this paper Turk's Head over something round and follow around with a thong until the working end comes back to the standing end. Tear off the paper Turk's Head and the leather one remains (Figs. 6 and 7).

Also, three thongs may be braided and tied together as shown in Figs. 8, 9 and 10, which will result in a Turk's Head of three parts and five bights. Similar experimentation is possible with other flat braids.

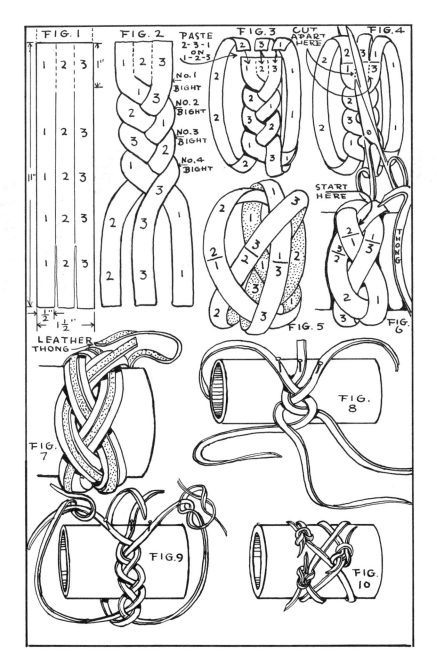

PLATE 46—Braided Paper Turk's Head.

PLATE 47

THREE-PART FIVE-BIGHT TURK'S HEAD—This is the regular free-hand method of tying the three-part five-bight Turk's Head, the same Turk's Head worked out in Plate 46 by braiding three thongs and then tying the ends together.

In Fig. 1 the thong has been passed over the mandrel with the standing end, A, at the left and the working end, B, inclined to the right. The working end, B, makes another complete circuit (Fig. 2) and when it comes back to the front as in Fig. 3 it passes under the standing end.

Now take the bight of the standing part as shown by the arrow-line in Fig. 4 and pull it beneath the bight to its left. Pass the working end, B, under and through this bight as indicated by the arrow-line in Fig. 5 and shown in Fig. 6. Turning the mandrel slightly to show the rear, pull the bight of the standing end under the bight to its right. The working end passes upward through this bight (Fig. 7) and around the mandrel to come up alongside the standing end (Fig 8). The knot is complete.

In Fig. 9 is shown a diagram pattern for making this Turk's Head. Place a piece of heavy wrapping paper beneath the page, and using a carbon, trace over the pattern. Be sure to trace all the circles shown on the pattern and the X marks shown in the bights.

At the top of the pattern, where indicated, cut the paper off flush. Then roll up the paper from the bottom end, having left it sufficiently long beyond the pattern at this end, until a cylinder is formed and the ends of the wavy lines on the pattern exactly meet.

Place a rubber band around the cylinder on the left side of the pattern, and then stick pins through the ten places in the bights marked with an X. Be sure all the lines at the ends come together.

With the standing end of the leather thong placed beneath the rubber band start laying the thong around the cylinder, following the line from the point marked "Start," and around the pins at the points marked X. The working end always passed *over* a thong except where there is a circle, in which cases it passes *under*.

When the point designated as *end,* is reached the knot is complete. Withdraw the pins, slip off the loose Turk's Head and adjust it over the lace where it is to be used. Then tighten it up by going completely over the knot from start to finish.

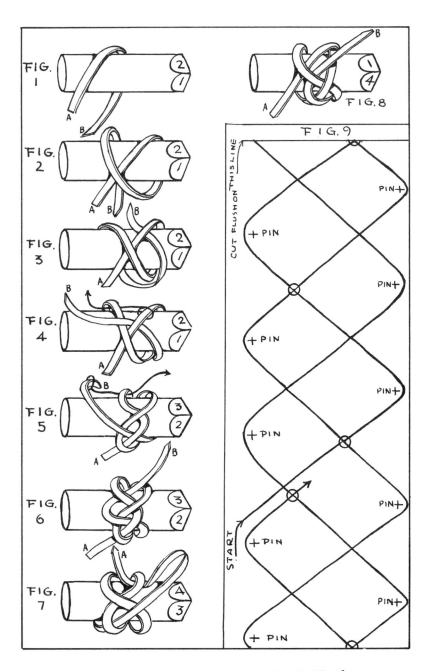

PLATE 47—Three-part Five-Bight Turk's Head.

PLATE 48

FIVE-PART FOUR-BIGHT TURK'S HEAD—Hold the mandrel (Fig. 1) so that the sections marked 1 and 4 are visible, with the figure 1 uppermost. Lay the standing part of the thong so that it covers these two sections and is well inclined to the right.

Pass the working end of the thong around the mandrel and back over its own part as in Fig. 1, after which it circles the mandrel again, inclined this time to the left. Bring it forward, beneath the standing end, with the working end in the area of section 1 (Fig. 2). The arrow-line in Fig. 2 indicates the next pass which is under the loop in section 1.

Draw the thong to the extreme left and under the mandrel bringing it up alongside and to the right of the standing part (Fig. 3). The arrow-line in Fig. 3 indicates how it follows parallel to the standing part under the thong in section 4.

The next pass is shown in Fig. 4 where the thong, still parallel to the standing part, has passed under one in section 4, over one at the bottom of section one, is inclined to the right and then passed over the standing part at the top of section 1. The arrow-line indicates its path under the next loop in back.

In Fig. 5 the mandrel is turned clockwise to illustrate section 2, with section 1 at the bottom. This shows how the thong passes under the loop indicated by the arrow-line in Fig. 4.

Now turn the mandrel back to its original position with sections 1 and 4 in view (Fig. 6). Observe that there is a path around the knot, in which one section of the thong goes over two, and another under two. The idea is to pass the end of the thong in such a manner that the complete knot will be in a sequence of over one, under one throughout, in other words, *lock* these sections.

The path is clearly shown by the arrow-line in Fig. 6. Pass the end over that part in section 4 and under that part in section 1 and the thongs will be locked so far as this part of the knot is concerned.

In Fig. 7 the end has been passed over one, under one, and over one and at the top there is a loop which is passed under two other parts, shown by the arrow-line. In Fig. 8 the mandrel is turned in a counter-clockwise direction so that sections 4 and 3 are in view, showing the bottom of the knot. Pass over one and under one, as shown by the arrow-line. The last and final move is indicated by the arrow-line in Fig. 9, when the working end is placed up alongside the standing end. The completed knot is shown in Fig. 10. A diagram pattern for this knot will be found on the next plate.

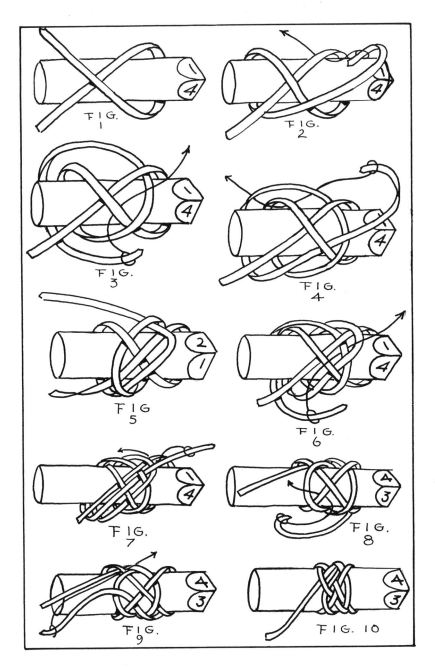

PLATE 48—Five-Part Four-Bight Turk's Head.

PLATE 49

LABYRINTH METHOD OF MAKING A FIVE-PART FOUR-BIGHT TURK'S HEAD—The theory behind this method is, that the more ways you learn to tie a Turk's Head the better. When completed by this procedure, it may readily be observed that each ring interlocks in an under-one-over-one-sequence.

It takes a comparatively long thong in relation to the final knot obtained, to tie the Turk's Head by this method so be sure to keep the kinks out of the thong and see that the hair side is always uppermost.

Start by laying the working end of the thong on a flat surface and making a loop in it as shown in Fig. 1. The next loop is indicated in this figure by the arrow-line.

In Fig. 2 this second loop has been made and the arrow-line indicates the third step. The letter X indicates in each case the center of the knot and where the mandrel will be if the knot is tied by the previous method in Plate 48.

In Fig. 3 the third step has been executed and the arrow-line shows the final phase of tying this intricate knot, which truly presents the aspect of a labyrinth. Attention should be called here to the *path* spoken of in the text for Plate 48. It is more clearly shown here just how, by passing the thong along it, the interlocking process of the knot is completed.

In Fig. 4 the working end has been brought up alongside the standing end and the knot is complete. A mandrel is inserted at the point marked X and the flat knot is carefully worked down to cylindrical shape by tightening along the arrows shown on the thong itself.

A diagram pattern for making this knot is given in Fig. 5. Follow the previous directions for making this knot by the fool-proof pattern method.

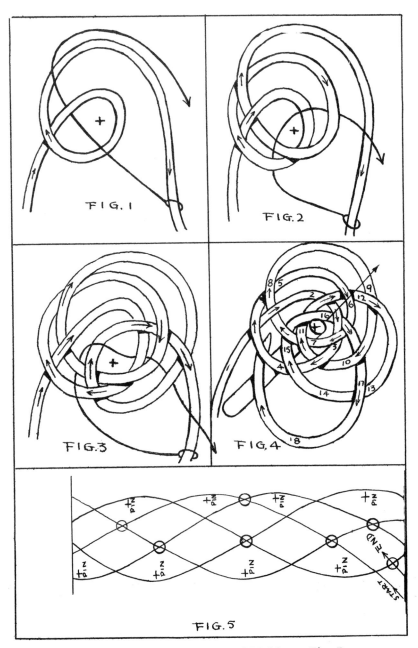

FIG. 1

FIG. 2

FIG. 3

FIG. 4

FIG. 5

PLATE 49—Labyrinth Method of Making a Five-Part
Four-Bight Turk's Head.

99

PLATE 50

FOUR-PART THREE-BIGHT TURK'S HEAD—Start this Turk's Head with the mandrel turned so that sections 1 and 4 are toward you, with section 1 uppermost.

Lay the thong on the mandrel so that it is in the area of sections 1 and 4 and the working end is inclined toward the right (Fig. 1).

Pass the thong around the mandrel, inclining it to the left as shown in Fig. 2. The arrow-line indicates the next move in which the thong is passed beneath two of its parts in the sections 1 and 4. Keep the loop of the thong extended to the right at the juncture of sections 1 and 4, although the working end, after passing under the second of its parts, is inclined to the left.

In Fig. 3 it is seen that the thong has passed beneath its two parts, with the loop inclined to the right. The arrow-line indicates the beginning of the final steps—the important interlocking steps.

Fig. 4 shows this first interlocking step. The thong has passed over one and under one in sections 4 and 1.

In Fig. 5 the mandrel has been turned toward you in a clockwise direction so that the back of the knot is visible. Here is another interlocking path of over-one-under-one sequence.

In Fig. 6 the working end has been brought up alongside the standing end and the Turk's Head is complete. Tighten the knot by working it carefully, beginning at the standing end and continuing around.

Fig. 7 is a diagram pattern of the four-part three-bight Turk's Head. Follow previous directions.

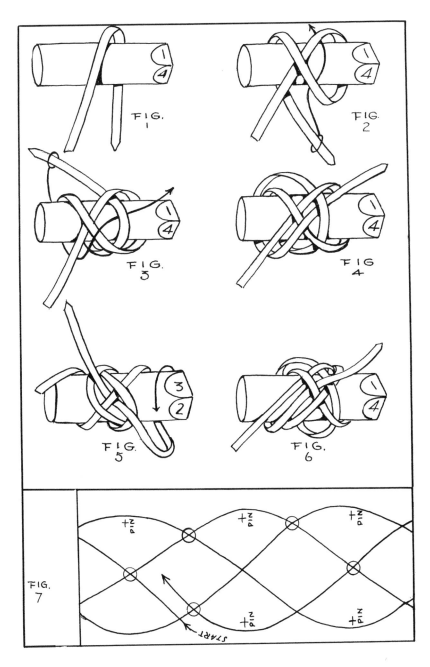

PLATE 50—Four-Part Three-Bight Turk's Head.

101

PLATE 51

SLIDING KNOT OR FIVE-PART TWO-BIGHT TURK'S HEAD—This is a relatively simple but very important Turk's Head. It is the key to some of the more intricate Spanish knots. In itself it is a valuable knot because it can be made over small diameters, thanks to its two bights, and yet is wide because of its five parts. Cowboys double and triple the knot to increase its width.

Begin with the mandrel turned so that sections 1 and 4 face you. Lay the standing part of the knot over the mandrel, covering these two sections (Fig. 1), the working end of the thong inclined to the right.

Turn the thong twice around the mandrel as in Fig. 2, spiraling it towards the left.

Pass the thong underneath the mandrel and to the front and then to the right and over the two spirals as indicated by the arrow-line in Fig. 2, and then pass it under the loop at the top of section 1.

Fig. 3 shows this step completed and indicates the next step by the arrow-line. Bring the thong down in the rear and up to the front between the two spiraled thongs. Here, by going over one and under one, the interlocking pass is accomplished.

The previously indicated step is illustrated in Fig. 4 and the arrow-line indicates the final step. Bring the thong to the extreme left, over one of its parts on the left and back up to the front alongside the standing part.

This completes the knot, unless it is desired to double it, in which case, continue as in Fig. 5. Start along the right side of the standing part and follow it with the thong, passing under when it passes under and over when it passes over. In other words, where there was originally one thong there will now be two. To triple, pass in the same way once more, following the two parallel thongs.

Enlarging Turk's Heads by doubling is a common practice, and in rope work, it actually beautifies the knot. But in leather work it is quite unsatisfactory, because the flat thongs overlap at the curves, giving the work an unfinished and uncouth appearance. When one becomes completely familiar with the Turk's Head knot in all its phases he will realize that there are Turk's Heads, as well as Spanish Knots, that can cover any surface, without the slightest necessity for doubling or tripling.

A diagram pattern for the sliding knot is given in Fig. 7.

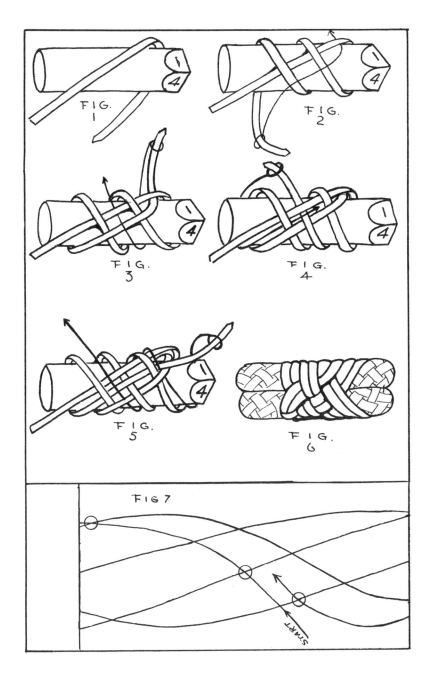

PLATE 51—Sliding Knot or Five-Part Two-Bight Turk's Head.

103

PLATE 52

FIVE-PART THREE-BIGHT TURK'S HEAD—This Turk's Head will assume an almost spherical form when tied and is, therefore, valuable as the covering for the handle end of canes, quirts and such. While it adapts itself to the circumference of the core, it also can be closed over the top by virtue of its three bights.

Hold the mandrel so that sections 1 and 4 are toward you, with section 1 uppermost. Lay the working end of thong so that it is within the area of sections 4 and 1 and inclined to the right as shown in Fig. 1.

In the next step bring it underneath toward the left and pass it completely around the mandrel again, the part in front inclined to the right, and the part in the back to the left, as shown in Fig. 2. It now passes over three of its own parts, the two in sections 4 and 1 and the other in the rear, without passing under any. Incline the thong far to the *left* or *top* side of the standing end as shown in Fig. 3. Pass it upward and over two of its own parts, to the left of the standing part and under the standing part at the top of the mandrel. This is indicated by the arrow-line in Fig. 3.

Fig. 4 shows the mandrel turned so that sections 4 and 3 are in view, illustrating the finished operation, and then the mandrel is turned back so that sections 1 and 4 face you, revealing the course of the working end of the thong. A path lies open along the arrow-line in Fig. 5, which, when followed by the thong, will interlock the parts as the over-one-under-one-over-one sequence is executed (Fig. 5).

With the mandrel again turned to sections 2 and 1 the end of this interlocking path will be seen. Pass the thong under one of its parts as in Fig. 6, then bring it around underneath, over one thong and alongside and to the right of the standing end (Fig. 6). The finished knot is shown in Fig. 7.

This knot can be followed around again to double it, and still again to triple it, as shown. There are better woven knots for this purpose, but for those who prefer the common practice it will serve when doubled or tripled. Be as careful as possible to keep the thongs from overlapping in doubling and tripling.

A diagram pattern is shown in Fig. 9.

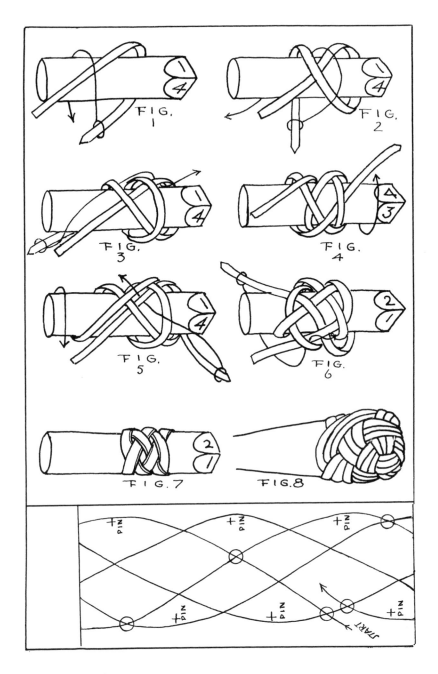

PLATE 52—Five-Part Three-Bight Turk's Head.

PLATE 53

SIX-PART FIVE-BIGHT TURK'S HEAD RAISED FROM A FOUR-PART THREE-BIGHT TURK'S HEAD—The four-part, three-bight Turk's Head shown in Plate 50 is the foundation upon which may be woven the larger knots of even parts. It can be raised to the six-part, five-bight Turk's Head and the six-part, five-bight can be raised to the eight-part, seven-bight Turk's Head and so on.

The key is given in this plate. Fig. 1 shows the four-part, three-bight Turk's Head tied according to the previous instructions. The numerals on the thong indicate in progressive order the course of the working end from the start to the finish.

First, place the working end of the thong alongside and to the right of the standing part (Fig. 1), allowing it to follow the right of the standing part to the top of the mandrel as indicated by the arrow-line in Fig. 1.

Now turn the mandrel as indicated by the curved arrow-line in Fig. 1, so that sections 3 and 2 are toward you, as shown in Fig. 2. The thong marked with the sequence number 2 is the standing part, and the working end, marked with a 6, passes *beneath* it and follows to its left, as indicated by the arrow-line in Fig. 2. Leave a small bight in the working end where it passes under the standing part.

Turn the mandrel back to the front so sections 1 and 4 are in view (Fig. 3). The arrow-line indicates the interlocking path in which the procedure is over one thong and under one.

Turning the mandrel again, so that sections 2 and 1 are toward you (Fig. 4), continue along this interlocking path passing over one and under one. This latter pass, indicated by the arrow-line in Fig. 4, shows the path of the working end beneath the bight which is left in Fig. 2, where the working end passed under the standing part.

Continue to turn the mandrel so that sections 3 and 2 are in view and the interlocking path is indicated by the arrow-line in Fig. 5. Pass over one, under one, over one and under one, each time locking the other parts of the thongs so their sequence also is over one, under one.

Turn the mandrel back to show sections 1 and 4 and bring the working end alongside and to the right of the standing end (Fig. 6). The completed knot is shown in Fig. 7. A diagram pattern is provided in Fig. 8. To raise the six-part to the eight-part, follow exactly the same procedure.

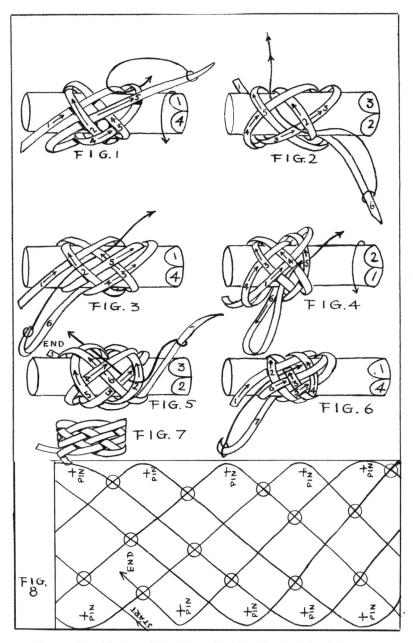

FIG. 1

FIG. 2

FIG. 3

FIG. 4

FIG. 5

FIG. 6

FIG. 7

FIG. 8

PLATE 53—Six-Part Five-Bight Turk's Head Raised from a
Four-Part Three-Bight Turk's Head.

107

PLATE 54

SEVEN-PART SIX-BIGHT TURK'S HEAD RAISED FROM A FIVE-PART FOUR-BIGHT TURK'S HEAD—Begin with the five-part, four-bight Turk's Head shown in Plate 48. Notice in Fig. 1, that the end of the standing part is numbered 1 and the working end is numbered 6. These are the progressive numbers denoting each move in making the original knot. They will be continued as the knot progresses.

The working end is alongside and to the right of the standing part (Fig. 1). The working end follows the course of the standing part, passing along to the right until the top of the knot is reached, as indicated in the arrow-line in Fig. 1.

In Fig. 2 the mandrel has been turned so that the rear is in view. This section of the standing part is numbered 2 and the working end passes over it (but under the same thong it passes under) and goes down to its left side. Fig. 2 indicates this pass and in Fig. 3 the next step is shown.

The working end is now back alongside the end of the standing part (Fig. 4). This time do not follow the path of the standing part, but where it goes *under* pass the working end *over*, and where it goes *over* pass the working end *under*. The first step is indicated in the arrow-line in Fig. 4. This shows the interlocking path which can easily be followed completely around the knot.

Turning the mandrel again, so that the rear shows, the arrow-line in Fig. 5 continues to follow this interlocking path, that is, under one, over one, under one, over one, under one and over one at the extreme left.

In Fig. 6, the working end is back at the start and this time the knot is finished when the working end is brought alongside the standing part as indicated by the arrow-line.

Tighten the knot by drawing on the thong from the start, and, following the sequence in which it was made, pull up the slack until the point shown in Fig. 6 is again reached. It may be necessary to go around several times to get it completely tight. Insert a little cement where the standing part and working part touch beneath the other portions of the thong, cut the ends off flush and tuck in.

To increase the seven-part to the nine-part follow the same procedure that was used to increase the five-part to the seven-part. This Turk's Head can be made as large as desired; each time it is raised increases it by two bights and two parts.

To make the seven-part, six-bight Turk's Head follow the diagram pattern in Fig. 7.

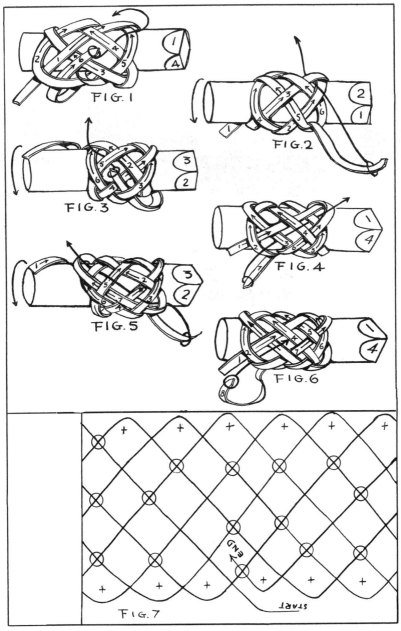

FIG. 1

FIG. 2

FIG. 3

FIG. 4

FIG. 5

FIG. 6

FIG. 7

PLATE 54—Seven-Part Six-Bight Turk's Head Raised from a
Five-Part Four-Bight Turk's Head.

PLATE 55

Two-Bight Turk's Head of any Length—By the following method you can make a Turk's Head any length you wish. The number of times the thong is wrapped about the mandrel in the beginning is the determining factor. When the thong is brought back toward the starting point, the number of times it touches the thong first wrapped around will determine the number of sections of the knot. If it touches twice, it will be a two-section knot, if three times, a three-section knot, etc.

Pass the thong around the mandrel three times toward the right (Fig. 1). The small numbers on the thong itself indicate its progress.

The arrow-line in Fig. 1 shows the second pass, which is already completed in Fig. 2. Now go around for the third time, in the direction indicated by the arrow-line in Fig. 2 and shown in Fig. 3. Up to this point the working end of the thong always passes over each of its parts.

Next, pass the working end beneath the outer part of the thong marked with the numeral 3 (Fig. 3). This is the beginning of the interlocking path. Close study will reveal this path spiraled around the mandrel, where one thong passes over two, the next under two and the next over two.

To *lock* these thongs pass over the thong which lies over two, and under the thong which is under two, as shown in Fig. 4. Continue in Fig 5, following the same pattern, over one, under one, over one, under one.

Having reached the extreme left-hand side (Fig. 6), pass over the thong there, then under one and finally over one. The working end now comes alongside the standing end (Fig. 7) and the knot is completed (Fig. 8).

This knot is sometimes doubled and not infrequently tripled. To do this, start following the standing part around and around, keeping on the same side of it all the time and passing *over* where it passes *over* and *under* where it passes *under*. This doubled knot is shown in Fig. 9. To triple go around and around again in the same fashion.

A diagram pattern is given in Fig. 10 for making the single knot.

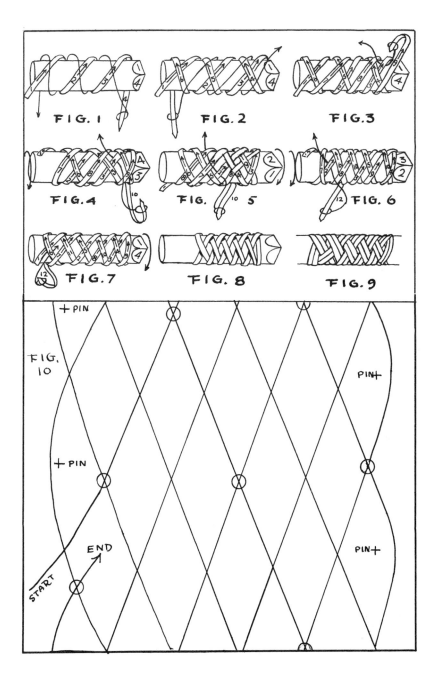

FIG. 1

FIG. 2

FIG. 3

FIG. 4

FIG. 5

FIG. 6

FIG. 7

FIG. 8

FIG. 9

FIG. 10

PIN

PIN

PIN

PIN

PIN

START

END

PLATE 55—Two-Bight Turk's Head of Any Length.

111

PLATE 56

Long Three-Bight Turk's Head—This knot is similar to the one in Plate 55, except that it has three instead of two bights. With three bights it can be used around a core of larger circumference. Remember, the greater the number of bights, the larger in diameter the knot will be; this is the reason why Turk's Heads are made with varied numbers of bights.

Wrap the thong around the mandrel twice and then bring it back over its own loop at the right and toward the left under the standing part as shown in Fig. 1.

Take another turn over the standing part and around the mandrel and bring the thong up alongside the standing part to the right side. It is passed to the right and goes under its own part in the center of the mandrel (Fig. 2).

Continue toward the right with the working end, pass over the outer loop and then back to the front and over this same loop again and also over the next thong as indicated by the arrow-line in Fig. 3.

Now pass the working end beneath the next two thongs, indicated by the arrow-line in Fig. 4 and shown in Fig. 5.

In Fig 6 the working end passes over the standing part and the extreme outer left-hand loop, indicated by the arrow-line in Fig. 7, and is brought to the front, this time to the *left,* or top, of the standing part. It goes over two thongs and under two thongs, indicated by the arrow-line in Fig. 7. In Fig. 8 it passes over the next two thongs and under the outer loop to the right, as indicated by the arrow-line.

Now the interlocking path can be seen, where the working end will first pass under the outer loop, over the next thong, under the next, over the next and under the next, going toward the left, of course. This path is indicated by the arrow-line in Fig. 9. Continue locking the thongs, over one, under one, over one and under the outer loop at the left (Fig 10). Bring the working end back, over one, and under the thong alongside the standing end and the knot is finished.

A diagram pattern is given in Fig. 12.

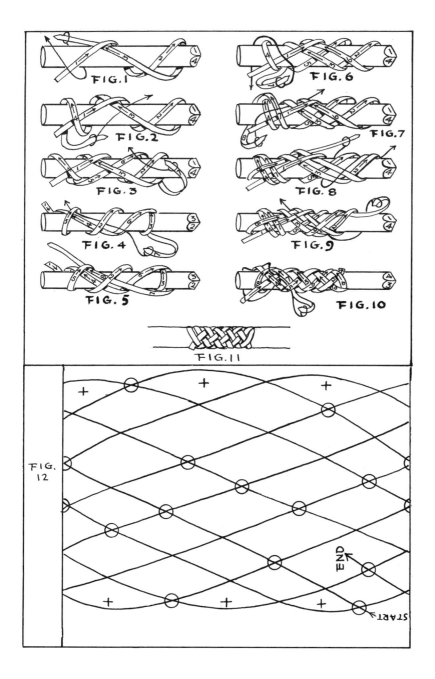

PLATE 56—Long Three-Bight Turk's Head.

113

PLATE 57

Woven Ring Knot of One Pass—This knot has as its foundation the three-part, five-bight Turk's Head shown in Plate 47. It will be the first example of how a Turk's Head skeleton is used in knot weaving.

In the drawings, the skeleton knot, the three-part, five-bight Turk's Head, is shown shaded, so the course of the braid can more easily be followed. In the finished three-part, five-bight Turk's Head of Plate 47 the working end is brought up alongside and to the right of the standing end.

In this knot the working end is withdrawn and passed *over* the standing end and up under one thong to the *left* or top of the standing end (Fig. 1).

In Fig. 2 the mandrel has been turned slightly to show the top, and now the working end passes over two thongs and under one and alongside the *right* of the standing part. One of the thongs passed over is the right-hand outer loop of the standing part.

In Fig. 3 the mandrel has again been turned, this time to show the bottom, and again the working end passes over two thongs. One of these thongs is the standing part and this pass brings the working end to the left-hand side of the standing part, as it passes to the right, indicated by the arrow-line in this figure.

The mandrel is turned back to its original position.

From now on the sequence is over two, under two. The fid is shown in Fig. 4 splitting the parallel thongs formed in the first pass when the working end went up alongside the left of the standing part. The working end of the thong follows this path opened by the fid.

In Fig. 5 the fid opens the path from the other side. The working end passes over two and under two (under the same two beneath which the fid passed). The next step (Fig. 6) shows the fid opening a path on the right. The working end follows this course and in Fig. 7 is brought up alongside and to the right of the standing part, and the knot is finished (Fig. 8).

A diagram pattern is given in Fig. 9.

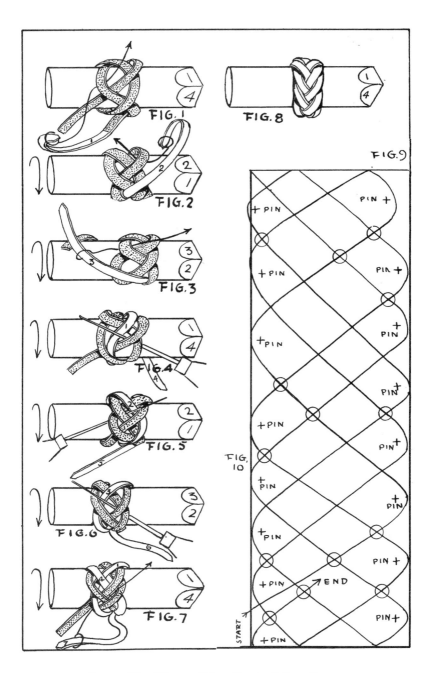

FIG. 1

FIG. 8

FIG. 2

FIG. 9

FIG. 3

FIG. 4

FIG. 5

FIG. 10

FIG. 6

FIG. 7

START

END

PLATE 57—Woven Ring Knot of One Pass.

PLATE 58

WOVEN RING KNOT OF THREE PASSES—Start with the woven ring knot of one pass shown in Plate 57. This knot is shown on the mandrel in Fig. 1. The standing end is designated as A and the working end as B.

With the working end, B, follow the path of the standing part, A. The arrow-line Fig. 1 illustrates how the working end is brought up alongside and to the left of the standing end.

In Fig. 2 the mandrel has been turned to show the back. Pass the working end, B, up alongside the left of the standing end and then over it, and at the same time under the two thongs as shown and to the right side of the standing end.

Again pass the working end, B, which is now to the right of the standing part, A, over the latter and follow it to the left side, indicated by the fid. In Fig. 3 the mandrel has been turned to illustrate this operation.

This completes one circuit of the knot, starting with the working end alongside the left of the standing part, then passing over it to its right side, then again over it to its left side, each time following the course the standing part takes, going under and over the same thongs as does the standing part.

In Fig. 4, where the working end and standing part are parallel, the fid has passed between them, separating them, thus providing a course for the working end, B.

The sequence from now on for the working end will be over three thongs and under three thongs, each time separating two parallel thongs.

Pass the fid beneath three thongs and split the parallel thongs, this time from the left-hand side, making an opening through which to pass the working end, B, as shown in Fig. 5.

Follow the same procedure on the right side, passing the fid beneath three thongs and splitting the parallel ones, as shown in Fig. 6. The working end, B, goes through this aperture.

In Fig. 7 the final move is shown. Bring the working end, B, up alongside the standing end, A and under the same three thongs and the knot is complete.

This knot can be made over a leather collar or even over another Turk's Head, such as the ordinary three-part, five-bight knot shown in Plate 47. This gives it a pleasing raised effect.

A diagram pattern to make the knot is given in Fig. 9.

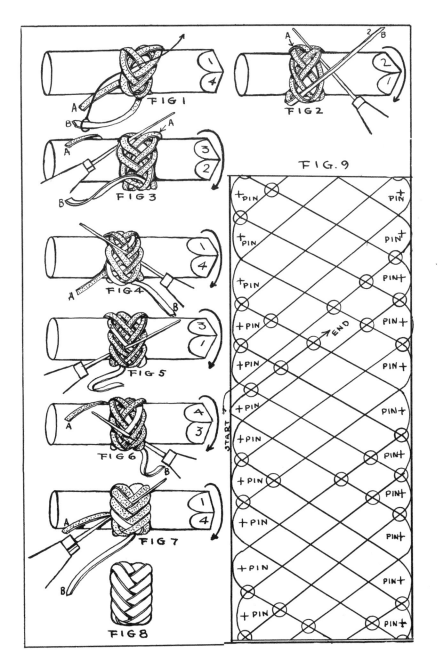

PLATE 58—Woven Ring Knot of Three Passes.

117

PLATE 59

GAUCHO KNOT OF ONE PASS—The Gaucho Knot of One Pass is in reality a nine-part eight-bight Turk's Head. But in this instance it is braided instead of tied in the usual way.

Use a mandrel with a leather collar as shown in Fig. 1. If this knot, or the other gaucho knots to follow, is used as a neckerchief slide, turn the leather collar so the smooth part is on the inner side, and work the knot over the flesh side. When the knot is finished slip the knot and collar off the mandrel and the smooth side of the collar will slide over the neckerchief.

The mandrel is numbered at the top so as to indicate when it has been turned. Start by laying the thong around the mandrel (and collar) as shown in Fig. 1. Pass the thong again to the rear and over the loop there bringing it to the front, where it passes under one and over one, (Fig. 2).

Now proceed as follows:

Rear: Under one, over one. (Fig. 3). Front: Over one, under one, over one (Figs. 4 and 5). Rear: Over one, under one, over one (Fig. 6).

Front: Under one, over one, under one, over one (shown by fid in Fig. 7). Rear: Under one, over one, under one, over one (shown by fid in Fig. 8).

Front: Over one, under one, over one, under one, over one, (shown by fid in Fig. 9). Rear: Over one, under one, over one, under one, over one (shown by fid in Fig. 10).

Front: Under one, over one, under one, over one, under one, over one (shown by fid in Fig. 11). Rear: Under one, over one, under one, over one, under one, over one (shown by fid in Fig. 12).

Front: Over one, under one, over one, under one, over one, under one, over one (indicated by fid in Fig 13). Rear: (The work is now moving around so the rear and front are practically one.) Over one, under one, over one, under one, over one, under one, over one (Fig. 14).

Front: Under one, over one, under one, over one, under one, over one, under one, over one (Fig. 15).

In the next move the working end comes up alongside the standing part and the knot is completed (Fig. 17). It should be understood, however, that the working end met the standing end several times before and at any of these points there would have been a complete knot.

In Fig. 18 is a diagram pattern for making this knot.

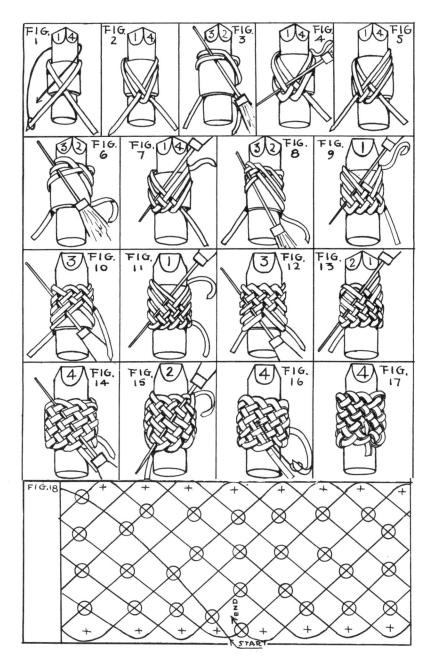

PLATE 59—Gaucho Knot of One Pass.

119

PLATE 60

Gaucho Knot of Two Passes—Made over the same type of leather collar as shown on the mandrel—a collar which can be slipped off with the knot—this knot provides an excellent neckerchief slide. If the knot is to be so used, the hair or smooth side of the leather collar should be *next* to the mandrel.

Begin as in Fig. 1 with the mandrel upright, and pass the thong around as shown. Then make another circuit, passing over the standing part, A, at all points (Fig. 2). Continue around again, going over both thongs in the rear, as shown in Fig. 3.

Start the braid by passing beneath the standing part, A, and over the next two thongs (Fig. 4). Do the same in the rear, (Fig. 5).

Now proceed as follows:

Front: Under two and over two (Fig. 6). Rear: Under two and over two (Fig. 7). Front: Over one, under two, over two (Fig. 8). Rear: Over one, under two, over two (Fig. 9). Front: Over two, under two, over two (Fig 10). Rear: Over two, under two, over two (Fig. 11).

Front: Under one, over two, under two, and over two (Fig. 12). Rear: Under one, over two, under two, and over two (Fig. 13).

Front: Under two, over two, under two and over two (Fig. 14).

In Fig. 15 the working end, B, comes up alongside the standing end, A, and Fig. 16 shows the finished knot.

A larger knot can be made with the same sequence of over-two-under-two, by continuing around from Fig. 15, passing under two, over two, under two and over two, then to the front, over one, under two, over two, under two and over two, and the same in the rear. This is the sequence followed in Fig. 9 except that there are now a larger number of thongs. To continue, follow the sequence in Fig. 10, which in this case would be over two, under two, over two, under two and over two. Keep on as in Figs. 11, 12, 13, 14 and 15 until the larger knot is finished.

A diagram pattern (Fig. 17) shows how to make the first knot.

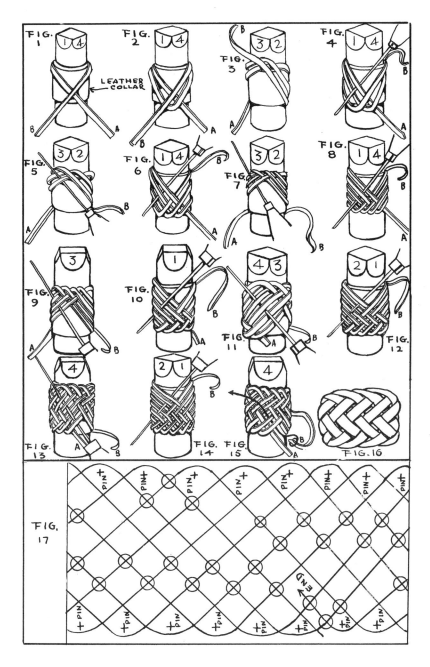

PLATE 60—Gaucho Knot of Two Passes.

121

PLATE 61

Gᴀᴜᴄʜᴏ Kɴᴏᴛ ᴏғ Tʜʀᴇᴇ Pᴀssᴇs—Two plates are necessary to illustrate adequately the manner of making this beautiful knot. So, upon completing the work demonstrated on this plate, (61), continue with Plate 61-A. Use an extra long thong and work carefully.

This knot is worked on a leather collar as were the two previous ones. As in the other cases, the collar can be turned so the smooth side is innermost, and the knot used as a neckerchief slide. The knot may also be used as a slide knot on lanyards, bridle reins, etc., not only to hold them together, but to adjust them to shorter or longer lengths and for decorative purposes.

Begin as in Fig. 1 by wrapping the thong around the mandrel (and collar) three times, always passing over each part of the thong.

In Fig. 2 make another turn, passing over the three thongs in the front and the rear as before. (Fig. 2 shows the back of the knot). We shall designate that part where the working end passes downward as the "front," and the opposite side of the mandrel where the working end passes upward as the "rear."

Here, then, is the sequence:

Front: Pass the working end under the first thong, which is the standing part, and (following the course of the fid as shown) the sequence will be, under one, over three (Fig. 3).

Rear: Under one, over three (Fig. 4).

Front: Under two, over three (Fig. 5).

Rear: Under two, over three. (Follow the course of the fid in Fig. 6).

Front: Under three, over three (Fig. 7). (This first move after passing under three completes a small knot, as the working end now meets the standing end. But continue to make the knot larger).

Rear: Under three, over three. (Follow the course of the fid in Fig. 8).

Front: Over one, under three, over three (Fig. 9).

Rear: Over one, under three, over three. (Follow the fid in Fig. 10).

Continue this sequence on the next plate.

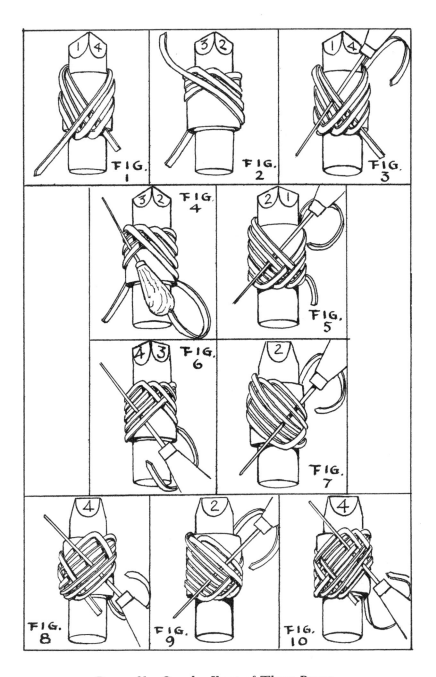

PLATE 61—Gaucho Knot of Three Passes.

123

PLATE 61-A

GAUCHO KNOT OF THREE PASSES (PART II)—To continue from the previous plate, pass the working end of the thong along the course taken by the fid in Fig. 11. This sequence is over two, under three and over three.

Rear: Over two, under three, over three (illustrated by the fid in Fig. 12).

By now it may be seen that the working end always makes the same pass in the rear as in the front. However, we shall continue to detail each move. Back to the sequence:

Front: Over three, under three, over three (Fig. 13).

Rear: Over three, under three, over three (Fig. 14).

Front: Under one, over three, under three, over three. (Follow the path of the fid in Fig. 15).

Rear: Under one, over three, under three, over three (fid in Fig. 16).

Front: Under two, over three, under three, over three (shown by fid in Fig. 17).

Rear: Under two, over three, under three, over three. (Illustrated by the course of the fid in Fig. 18. The knot is closing up now).

Front: Under three, over three, under three, over three (fid in Fig. 19).

Rear-front: Bring the working end around and under three, which places it alongside the standing end and completes the knot (Fig. 20). The finished knot is shown in Fig. 21.

This knot can be enlarged still further by continuing around. When the front is reached, again pass over one, under three, over three, and the same applies in the rear. When the point is reached where the pass is over three, under three, over three, under three, over three; start with under one, over three, under three, over three, under three and over three. Continue until an under three, over three, under three, over three and over three sequence is reached. When the working end comes alongside the standing end, the knot is completed.

A diagram pattern for making this interesting knot is shown in Fig. 22.

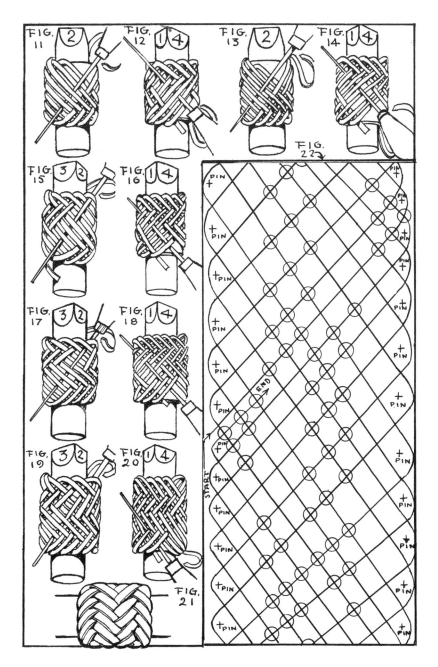

PLATE 61-A—Gaucho Knot of Three Passes (Part II).

PLATE 62

DOUBLE GAUCHO KNOT OF TWO PASSES—In the two-bight knot of any length (Plate 55) the number of crossings the thong made on its second pass indicated the number of sections of the knot. If it crossed twice it formed a two-section knot, if three times a three-section knot, and so on.

The same rule also holds in this knot. It is a two-section or double knot having an over-two-under-two sequence, the same as the one-section gaucho knot of two passes (Plate 60). It can be made in three sections, or four sections, etc., by crossing, on the second move, three thongs, four thongs, or as many as desired.

It will be necessary to demonstrate this knot in two plates, so the work will continue on Plate 62-A.

Start as in Fig. 1, by wrapping the thong around one and one-half times and bringing it back, passing the working end over its own part twice. Do this once more, as indicated in Figs. 2 and 3, never passing *under,* but always *over* each thong. Go around once more, inclining to the right as in Fig. 4, and then pass under one thong and over two as in Fig. 5. This is the beginning of the braid.

In the section of the knot on the left illustrated in Fig. 6, pass again under one and over two. In working to the right, repeat this in the left-hand section, under one, over two (Fig. 7), and again in the right-hand section, under one, over two (Fig. 8).

Now proceed as follows:

Under two, over two (Fig. 9). Under two, over two (Fig. 10). Under two, over two (Fig. 11).

In Fig. 11, after passing under two, (as indicated by the fid) a completed knot is shown, as the working end here meets the standing end. This makes a finished small knot, but can be enlarged in the following manner. Continue as in Fig. 12, under two, over two.

Now pass over one, under two, over two (Fig 13). Over one, under two, over two (Fig. 14). Over one, under two, over two (Fig. 15).

For instructions on completing this knot, turn to the next plate, 62-A.

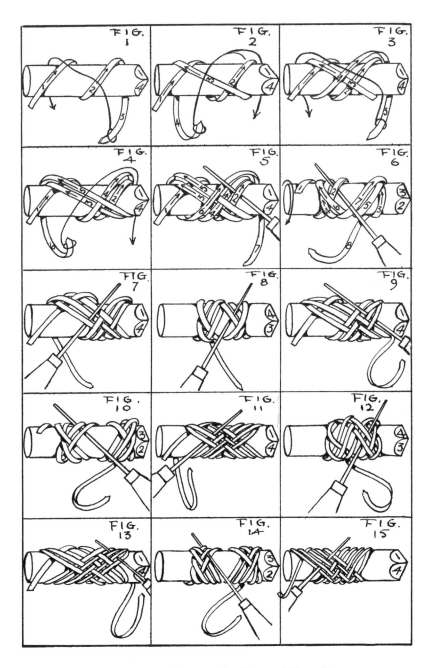

PLATE 62—Double Gaucho Knot of Two Passes.

127

PLATE 62-A

Continue the double gaucho knot of two passes in Fig. 16, by passing over one thong, under two thongs and over two. Then pass over two, under two and over two (Fig. 17).

Next, in the left-hand section, pass over two, under two and over two, indicated by the path of the fid in Fig. 18. (It will be noted here in combining the sequences of Figs. 17 and 18 that in the middle of the knot the working end actually passes over four thongs. This may look wrong but it will adjust itself in the over-two-under-two sequence as the work proceeds).

Continue as follows:

Back toward the right, over two, under two, over two (Fig. 19).

Over two, under two, over two (Fig. 20).

Toward the left, under one, over two, under two, over two (Fig. 21).

Under one, over two, under two, over two (Fig. 22).

Toward the right, under one, over two, under two, over two (Fig. 23).

Under one, over two, under two, over two (Fig. 24).

Toward the left, under two, over two, under two, over two (Fig. 25).

Under two, over two, under two, and over two (Fig. 26).

In Fig. 27, after passing under two thongs, the work comes back to the starting point and the working end is alongside the standing end, so the knot is complete. However, as with the other gaucho knots made by this braiding process, it may be continued around again and again, each time terminating at the point where working end and standing end meet. This will result in a knot with a greater number of bights, which will fit over a larger circumference and still close up when tightened. The finished knot is shown in Fig. 28.

Fig. 29 provides a diagram pattern for this knot.

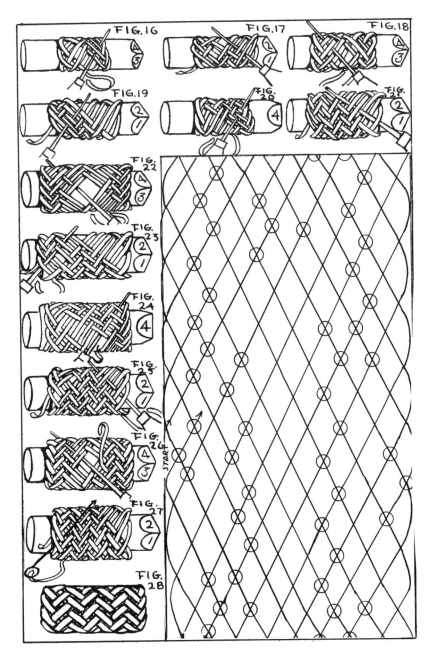

PLATE 62-A—Double Gaucho Knot of Two Passes (Continued).

129

PLATE 63

DOUBLE GAUCHO KNOT OF THREE PASSES—To make the double gaucho knot of three passes, wrap the thong around the mandrel two and one-half times. Then continue until at the right there are four thongs alongside each other, all of which have been passed over the top in going around. The sequence now is this:

To left (Fig. 1): Under one, over three in the right-hand section; under one, over three in the left-hand section.

To right: Under one, over three in the left-hand section; under one, over three in the right-hand section.

To left: Under two, over three, and again under two, over three.

To right: Under two, over three, and under two and over three.

To left: Under three, over three; under three, over three. (The next move where the working end meets the standing end, completes a small knot. But we shall continue to make a larger knot).

To right: Under three, over three; under three, over three.

To left: Over one, under three, over three; over one, under three and over three.

To right: Over one, under three, over three; over one, under three, over three.

To left: Over two, under three, over three; over two, under three, over three.

To right: Over two, under three, over three; over two, under three, over three.

To left: Over three, under three, over three; over three, under three, over three.

To right: Over three, under three, over three; over three, under three, over three.

To left: Under one, over three, under three, over three; under one, over three, under one, over three, under three, over three.

To right: Under one, over three, under three, over three; under one, over three, under three, over three.

To left: Under two, over three, under three, over three; under two, over three, under three, over three.

To right: Under two, over three, under three, over three; under two, over three, under three, over three. Then pass to the left under three, over three, under three, over three; under three, over three, under three, over three.

The next move is under three, with the working end alongside the standing end, and the knot is finished (Fig. 2).

In using this pattern it is best to work it with 3/32 inch commercial lacing and a thonging or lacing needle. Be very careful the ends of the pattern lines are true and coincide.

A diagram pattern is given in Fig. 3.

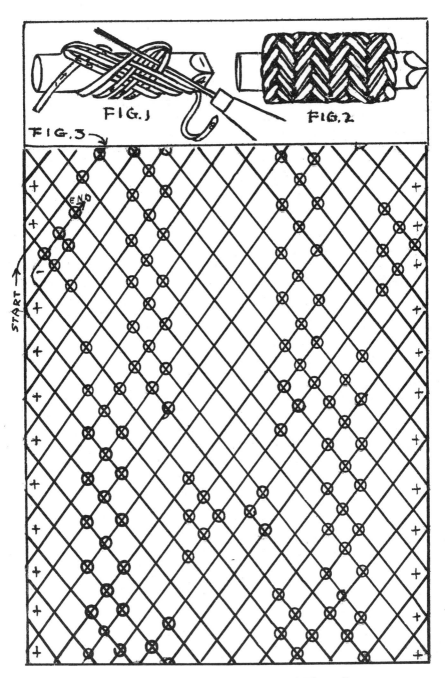

FIG.1

FIG.2

FIG.3

END

START

PLATE 63—Double Gaucho Knot of Three Passes.

PLATE 64

HERRINGBONE KNOT—This is a very dressy and decorative knot for the top of a quirt handle. It can be woven on any of the Turk's Heads having uneven parts, such as the five-part, seven-part, nine-part, etc. This particular knot will be made with the five-part, four-bight Turk's Head as the skeleton knot. While the five-part four-bight Turk's Head can be tied as shown in Plate 48, we will be consistent and weave it.

Wrap the thong around the mandrel (with collar) in the manner shown in Fig. 1. On the second turn pass it under the standing part (Fig. 1), and in the rear pass it under one and over one (Fig. 2).

Continue as follows:

Front: Over one, under one, over one (Fig. 3).

Rear: Over one, under one, over one (Fig. 4).

Front: Under one, over one, under one, over one (Fig. 5). This brings it back to the start, with the working part meeting the standing part (Fig. 6).

Now, instead of tucking it under one thong alongside and to the right of the standing part, tuck it under the standing part and under that thong which is looped over the standing part and up alongside the *left* of the standing part (Fig. 7), so that it follows the standing part upward, passing over one thong and under one thong (Fig. 7).

Pass the working end to the other side of the standing part beneath it and also beneath the thong on top of the standing part (Fig. 8).

With the working end follow the standing part down on its other side, passing under the same thong the standing part does (Fig. 9).

At the bottom of the knot in Fig. 10 the working end has returned to the point where it first passed along to the left of the standing part. Now pass it over the standing part and under its own part, as well as under the two adjacent thongs at the point where they cross each other. In other words the sequence is over one, under three.

Pass the working end upwards, following to the left of the thong on its right, until it reaches the top, where it goes over one thong and under three, as indicated by the arrow-line in Fig. 11. The braiding sequence is continued on the next plate 64-A.

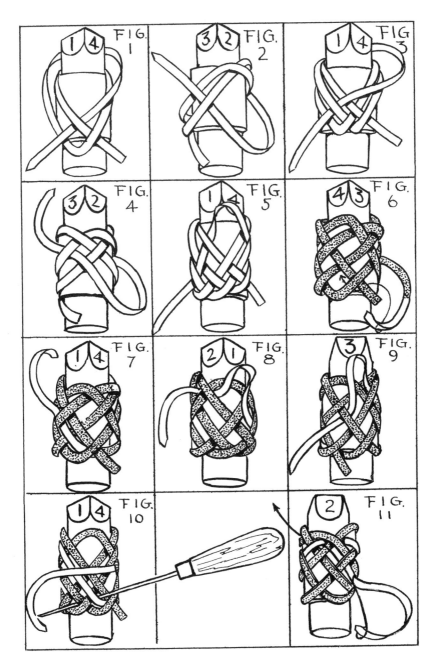

PLATE 64—Herringbone Knot.

133

PLATE 64-A

The last step in Plate 64 reached the top of the knot and the next pass will *split* two of the parallel thongs. Bring the working end down over one, under one, over two and under three, drawing it out at the bottom to the left as shown in Fig. 12.

Going up, the working end passes over one, under one, over two and under three, emerging at the top and left (Fig. 13).

Passing downward, the working end goes over one, under two, over two and under three, emerging at the bottom left (Fig. 14). (Note: Watch the numbers at the top of the mandrel which show when it has been turned).

Going up, the working end passes over one, under two, over two and under three, emerging at the top left (Fig. 15).

Fig. 16: Going down, the working end passes over two, under two, over two and under one (Fig. 16).

Fig. 17 shows the finish of the knot. Pass under two more thongs, including the standing part, and the knot is complete. This last pass could have been included in the previous one and the working end could have been brought under all three thongs at once. However, for the sake of clarity in instructions it is here done the longer way.

Both the shaded thongs and the white thongs in the completed knot (Fig. 18) represent a five-part, four-bight Turk's Head. In other words this complete knot is simply the result of weaving or interweaving these two Turk's Heads together.

The same type of knot can be made with a seven-part, six-bight Turk's Head, which would be the result of interweaving two seven-part Turk's Heads together. Also it can be made from the nine-part, eight-bight Turk's Head and so on.

It might be of interest here to say that Turk's Heads and woven knots have engaged the attention of many profound mathematicians and a ponderous literature has been written on them. They follow rules as inviolate as those of the planets, and the winding and intricate, even labyrinthine, twistings can be calculated to a nicety.

A diagram pattern for this knot is given in Fig. 19.

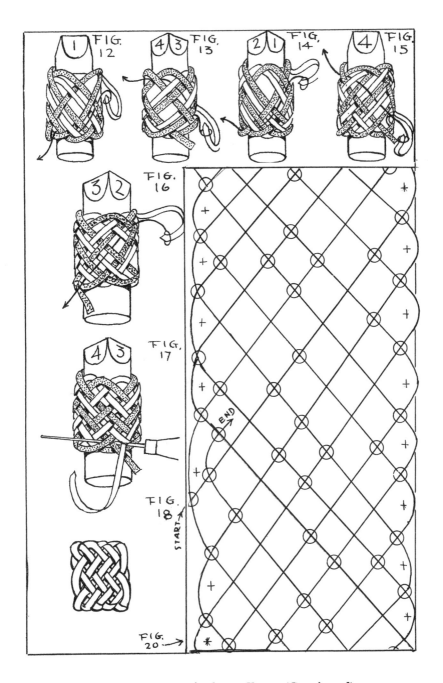

PLATE 64-A—Herringbone Knot (Continued).

135

PLATE 65

HEADHUNTER'S KNOT OF TWO PASSES—The man who first introduced the headhunter's knot to civilization never told how it was made. As the story goes, a chieftain of a savage tribe had explained to him how to braid the knot and then warned him that he would suffer dire consequences if he gave away the secret. However, as I have worked it out myself I am violating no confidence and fear no savage vengeance.

Start as in Fig. 1 by wrapping the thong around the mandrel (with leather collar). When the working end reaches the rear (the mandrel has been turned in Fig. 2 to show this) it passes *beneath* the thong there. This is the secret of the knot.

Proceed as follows:

Front: Over two (Fig. 3).

Rear: Under two (Fig. 4). (From now on always pass *over* the last two in front and *under* the last two in the rear).

Front: Under one, over two (Fig. 5).

Rear: Over one, under two (Fig. 6).

Front: Under two, over two (Fig. 7).

Rear: Over two, under two (Fig. 8).

Front: Over one, under two, over two (Fig. 9).

Rear: Under one, over two, under two (Fig. 10).

Front: Over two, under two, over two (Fig. 11).

In Fig. 12 the working end comes up under two thongs and alongside the standing end which, by our mathematical law, completes the knot. The finished knot is shown in Fig. 13.

If a larger knot is desired, keep passing around, varying the sequence at the top and bottom each time so that when working from the top down, the working end always comes out over the last two thongs, and when working up in the rear, the business end of the thong passes *under* the last two. When the working end comes up alongside the standing end the knot is finished. This is true, we repeat, of all the knots of this fascinating series.

A diagram pattern for this knot is provided in Fig. 13.

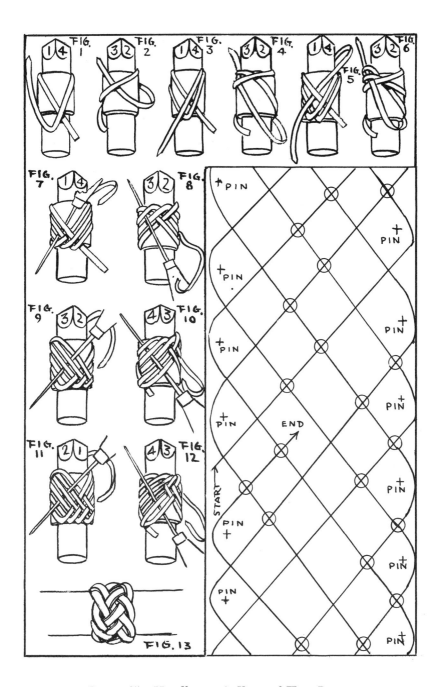

PLATE 65—Headhunter's Knot of Two Passes.

137

PLATE 66

HEADHUNTER'S KNOT OF THREE PASSES—As a headhunter's knot of over-three-under-three sequence, this may evoke a *triple* curse from the chief of the cannibal tribe for revealing the secret. But here goes:

Fig. 1 illustrates the same rule that was given in the beginning of the headhunter's knot of two passes (Plate 65), that is, the working end passes on top of all the thongs in the front and *beneath* all the thongs in the rear. The rear is not shown in Fig. 1 but all the thongs there go under each other.

Start by passing under one thong and over three (Fig. 1). Then to the rear (the mandrel has been turned to show) in Fig. 2 and pass over one and *under* three. The sequence from now on is:

Front: Under two, over three.
Rear: Over two, under three.
Front: Under three, over three.
Rear: Over three, under three.
Front: Over one, under three, over three.
Rear: Under one, over three, under three.
Front: Over two, under three, over three.
Rear: Under two, over three, under three.
Front: Over three, under three, over three.
Rear: Under three. The working end is now alongside the standing end and the knot is finished.

The completed knot is shown in Fig. 3.

If desirable to enlarge the knot, continue from this point with an under three, over three, under three sequence and when the front is again reached, pass under one, over three, under three, over three. The rear this time will be over one, under three, over three, under three.

Keep going in this manner, being sure that in the front the working end passes *over* the last three thongs and in the rear it passes *under* the last three thongs.

The savage tribes of the Philippines use split bamboo and weave this knot into finger rings. They also use it to adorn their spears and other warlike implements.

A diagram pattern for the over-three-under-three headhunter's knot is given in Fig. 4.

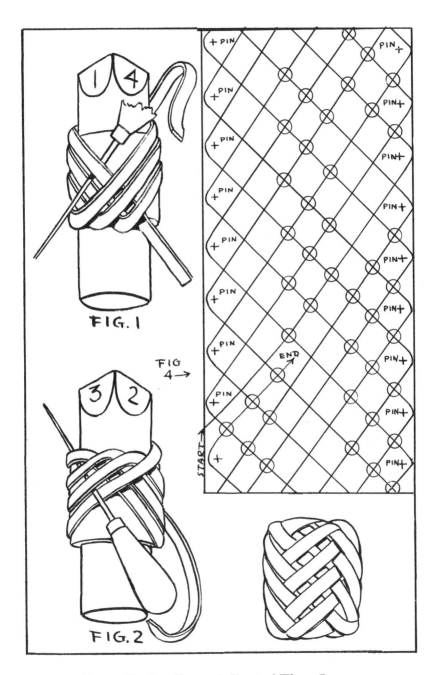

PLATE 66—Headhunter's Knot of Three Passes.

139

PLATE 67

PINEAPPLE OR GAUCHO BUTTON KNOT—Where the Herringbone Knot (Plate 64) was an interweave of two Turk's Heads of the same number of parts and bights, the Pineapple Knot is an interweave of two Turk's Heads of the same number of bights but different number of parts.

In this case, the basic or skeleton knot is a seven-part, six-bight Turk's Head and the one interwoven is a Turk's Head of five parts and six bights. This knot is usually made over a rounded core and also can be used on the heads of canes and quirts. It has, because of its double row of staggered bights at each end, the faculty of closing completely over a round surface.

If tightened around a small spherical core it makes a beautiful button. Also, the interweaving thong can be of a different tone or color, which gives a very unusual pattern.

The knot can be made any size or length, however, it should be made on a skeleton knot of uneven parts, such as the five-part, seven-part, nine-part, etc. A longer one can be made by interweaving the double or triple section basket-weave Turk's Head.

In Fig. 1 is shown the start of the basic, or skeleton knot. It illustrates a Turk's Head of five parts and four bights which will be raised to one of seven parts and six bights. Tie the five-part, four-bight Turk's Head as shown in Plate 48. Beginning at the front of the knot (Fig. 1), pass the working end, along parallel to the standing end, on its right, under one, over one, under one, over one.

At the top, working down (Fig. 2) pass over one, under one, over one, under one and over one (the bottom loop). The working end passing down in this last step was to the *left* of the standing part.

In Fig. 3, pass upward, again to the right of the standing end, over one, under one, over one, under one, over one and under one (top loop.) Follow the interlocking path downward, over one, under one, over one, under one, over one (Fig. 4).

This portion of the knot is shaded in Fig. 5. Begin with the unshaded part of the working end in Fig. 5, again follow alongside upward and to the right of the standing end, under one, over one, under one, over one, and then pass toward the left under the two thongs which cross each other.

Fig. 6: Down, over one, under one, over one, and under two (where the two thongs cross). Fig. 7: Work up, over one, under one, over one and under *three* where the working end divides two parallel thongs. Fig 8: Work down, over one, under one, over one and under three, splitting a pair.

Fig. 9: (Not shown clearly in the drawing) work up, over one, under one, over one, and under three (splitting a pair).

The sequence is continued on Plate 67-A.

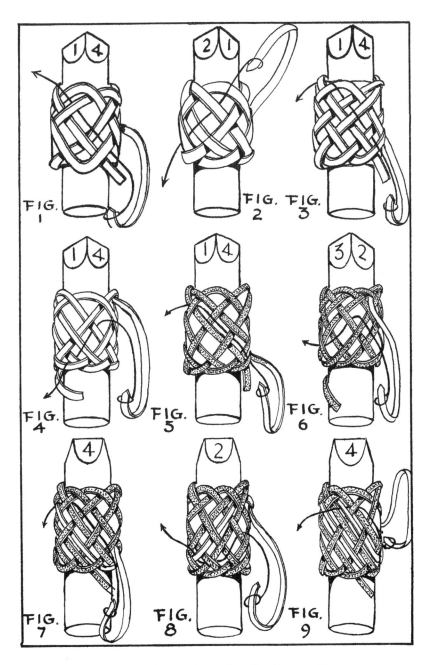

PLATE 67—Pineapple or Gaucho Button Knot.

141

PLATE 67-A

Continue the sequence of the Pineapple Knot; pass down (Fig. 10) over two (splitting a pair), under one, over one, and under three, splitting another pair.

Fig. 11: Pass up, over two (dividing a pair), under one, over one and under three. The last move splits a pair of parallel thongs.

Fig. 12: Pass down, over two (splitting a pair), under two (splitting a pair), over one and under three. This last move divides another pair.

Fig. 13: Proceed upward, over two (dividing a pair), under two (dividing another pair), over one, under three (splitting a third pair).

Fig. 14: Over two (dividing a pair), under two (dividing another pair), over two (splitting a third pair) and then under three (dividing a fourth pair).

Fig. 15: Pass up, over two (dividing a pair), under two (dividing a second pair), over two (dividing a third pair), and under three (splitting a fourth pair).

Fig. 16: Pass down, over two (splitting a pair), under two (splitting a second pair), over two (splitting a third pair), and then under three, bringing the working end alongside its own original part. The finished knot is shown in Fig. 17.

A diagram pattern is provided in Fig. 18.

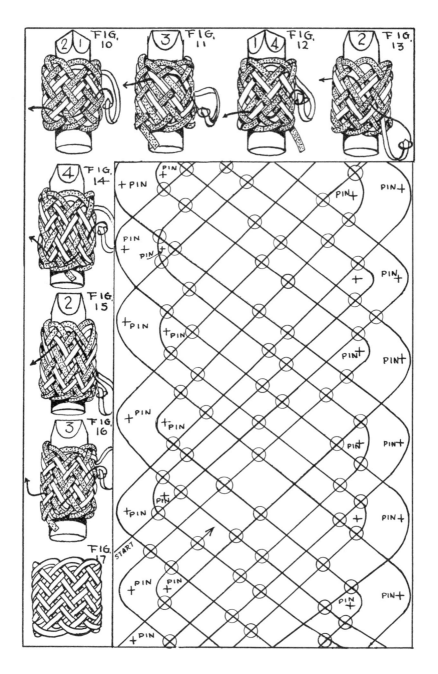

PLATE 67-A—Pineapple or Gaucho Button Knot (Continued).

143

PLATE 68

Ring Knot of Four Passes—This attractive knot must be used on a collar which will keep its outer edges or bights even.

Wrap the thong around the mandrel (with leather collar) four times, passing over the thongs in both front and rear. Then bring it around a fifth time as in Fig. 1 and pass the working end beneath the first thong, which is the standing part. Pass it over the last four.

In Fig. 2 the mandrel has been turned to show the rear. Pass the working end under one thong and over four.

Back to the front again in Fig. 3. Pass the working end under two thongs and over four.

In the rear (Fig. 4) make the same pass under two and over four.

Returning to the front (Fig. 5), now pass under three thongs and over four.

The knot is closing and front and rear are almost one in Fig. 6. Bring the working end up under three thongs and over four.

Bring the working end to the front and pass it under four thongs (Fig. 7). It is alongside the standing part in the next move (Fig. 8). The knot is completed (Fig. 9).

This knot can be made by wrapping the thongs around five times in the beginning and then the sixth time before the weaving is started. In such case, always pass over the last five thongs in both front and rear. It can be made also with an over-six-under-six or an even greater sequence, but it soon gets out of hand.

As cautioned in the beginning, when used on a quirt, whip, hackamore, cane or as a neckerchief slide knot, always work it over a collar so that the edges will not draw inward beneath the knot when it is tightened.

This knot is the last of the Turk's Heads and woven knots. In most cases they are basic and the braider can use the principles explained to experiment on his own. Hundreds of variations can be made and soon he will be a member of that exclusive cult of Turk's Head addicts.

Fig. 10 provides a diagram pattern for the Ring Knot of Four Passes.

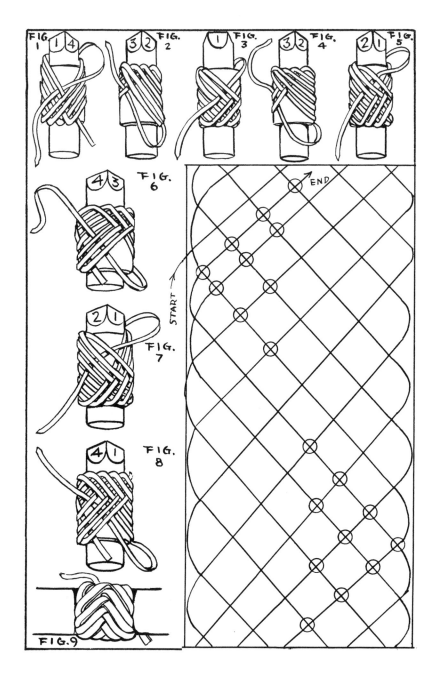

PLATE 68—Ring Knot of Four Passes.

PLATE 69

STAIRSTEP APPLIQUE OF ONE THONG—Like edge lacing, applique handicraft is both practical and beautiful. It is useful in joining pieces of leather and at the same time is pleasing to the eye. With the proper use of thong appliqué no thread or metal brads will ever be necessary. And it is needless to say that there is a harmonious relationship between a leather thong and the leather it joins and whose beauty it complements.

One of the simplest forms of appliqué is the stairstep type. It can be used not only in joining leather pieces at the edges, but also as a means of decoration in itself by following a pattern, such as initials or some particular design.

Space the holes the width of the thong. Enter the thong from the back through hole 1 (Fig. 1). Then pass it through hole 2 from the front (Fig. 1) and up and back through hole 1 from the rear (Fig. 2). Always be sure it consistently emerges either to the right or left of the portion of the thong already in the hole or slit. In this case it is always on the right.

Now bring the working end of the thong down from hole 1 to hole 3 and pass it through from the front to the back (Fig. 3). Pass it up from the back through hole 2, to the right of both thongs at that point (Fig. 4).

Next pass the thong down through hole 4 from the front (Fig. 5) and up through hole 3 (Fig. 6). Keep it to the right. Then down through hole 5 (Fig. 7), and so on in the same order until the finish.

In Fig. 9 is shown a diagram of how the braid looks from the rear. There are several variations of this attractive braid, which will be detailed later.

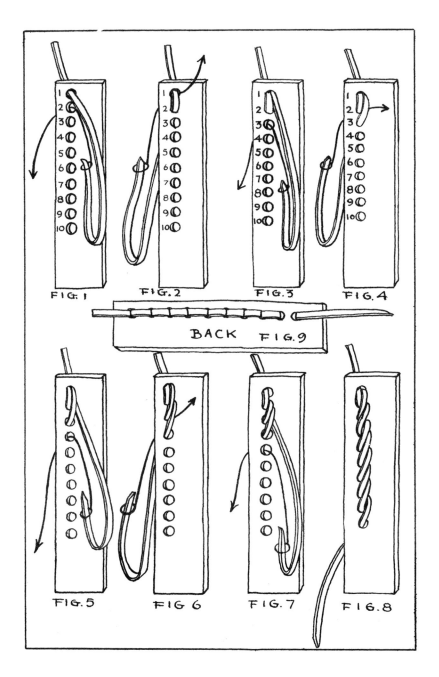

FIG. 1   FIG. 2   FIG. 3   FIG. 4

BACK   FIG. 9

FIG. 5   FIG 6   FIG. 7   FIG. 8

PLATE 69—Stairstep Appliqué of One Thong.

PLATE 70

TWO-THONG FOUR-PART APPLIQUE—As this is built upon the stairstep appliqué (Plate 69), first make the stairstep braid. Then, with a second thong, this one of a different color if desired, pass through the first hole at the top from the rear to the front as shown in Fig. 1. The original thong of the stairstep appliqué is white and the second thong is shown as shaded in the drawing.

Pass the shaded, or working thong over the white thong between holes 1 and 2, under the white thong to its right, then over the next and down through hole 3, from the front to the rear, as indicated by the arrow-line in Fig. 1

Now bring the working thong back up through hole 2 from the rear to the front and on the left side, indicated by the arrow-line in Fig. 2.

Next pass the working thong over one thong, under one and over one, then through hole 4, illustrated in Fig. 3. Bring it back again from the rear to the front through hole 3, to the left, as indicated by the arrow-line in Fig. 4.

The next step is the same as the preceding ones. Pass the working thong over one, under one, and over one, always inclined to the right, and then down through hole 5 (Fig. 5).

In the rear view (Fig. 6) it can be seen that the thongs overlap, as the shaded or working thong is brought through a hole on one side and up through a hole on the other side.

The finished work is shown in Fig. 7. This gives a pleasing, two-toned effect, but it can also be worked effectively with thongs of the same color. The braid simulates, after a fashion, the four-thong flat braid.

This type of thonging is very popular among leather braiders in Switzerland. It can be made with thongs of different widths; usually the original stairstep appliqué foundation is made of the wider thongs. It is an effective trimming on belts and other articles, although it must not be forgotten that it has the utilitarian value, as does all appliqué braiding, of joining together two or more pieces of leather.

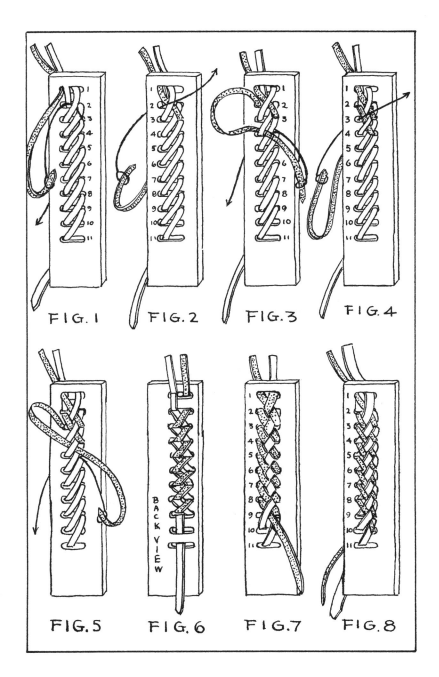

PLATE 70—Two-Thong Four-Part Appliqué.

PLATE 71

STAIRSTEP APPLIQUE OF TWO THONGS—This is similar to the stairstep appliqué of one thong (Plate 69) except that a closer braid is obtained by the use of two thongs.

It is used for joining pieces of leather and at the same time for decoration. A contrasting color to the leather base may be used to give a pleasing effect. Different leathers, such as goatskin thonging lace on cowhide or calfskin are quite effective.

To begin, insert the thong designated as B in the top hole from rear to front. Next, pass the one designated as A through the second hole from the rear to the front and under B (Fig. 1). In this drawing the arrow-line indicates the course of thong B. Pass it through the second hole from front to rear and to the left of thong A.

Now bring thong B forward through the third hole and inclined to the right, indicated by the arrow-line in Fig. 2. Pass thong A down through the third hole over thong B and to its left in the hole. Follow the arrow-line in Fig. 3.

In Fig. 4 the next move is indicated. Bring thong A from back to front through the fourth hole and inclined to the right. Pass thong B down over thong A and through the fourth hole from front to back and to the left of thong A at that point (Fig. 5).

When the two thongs are in the position shown in Fig. 6, tighten by pulling on both at the same time. Bring thong B back up through the fifth hole and incline it to the right.

Pass thong A down through the fifth hole over thong B and to its left in the hole (Fig. 7). The finished braid is shown in Fig. 8.

A back view of this braid is illustrated in Fig. 9 and resembles in every way the single thong braid.

Make the holes with a punch or with a small thonging chisel. The symmetry of the braid depends on the care used in spacing the holes evenly. When using slits made by a thonging chisel, always enlarge them with the fid before inserting the thonging end. Braid made with slits is much neater than when made with holes.

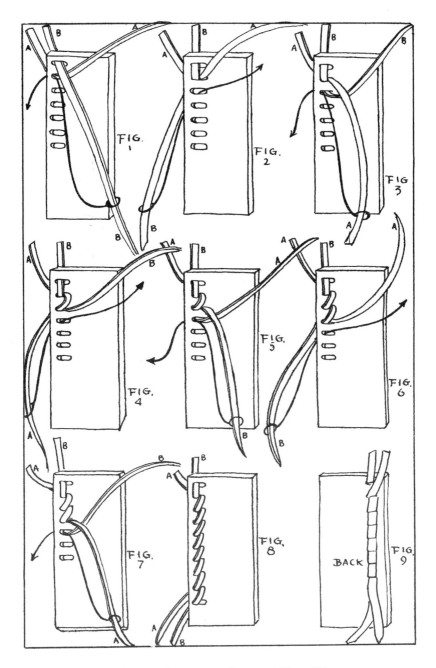

PLATE 71—Stairstep Appliqué of Two Thongs.

151

PLATE 72

CHAIN APPLIQUE OF ONE THONG—Pass the thong through the top hole from the rear to the front and down through the third hole as shown in Fig. 1. The arrow-line in this drawing indicates its path which is up through the second hole from the rear to the front and to the *right* of the standing part.

Next pass it down through hole 4 from the front to the rear.

Pass the working end up through hole 3, this time to the *left* of the standing part, as shown by the arrow-line in Fig. 2. Then bring it down through the fifth hole from the front to the rear.

Now bring it up through hole 4, this time to the *right* of the standing part, as indicated by the arrow-line in Fig. 3, and down through the sixth hole from the front to the rear. Continue thus, first passing back to one side of the standing part and next to the other side.

SPLIT-THONG APPLIQUE—This provides a double security in joining two pieces of leather and also gives a pleasing effect. First pass the thong through hole 1 from the rear to the front and down through hole 3 (Fig. 5). Now, in that part of the loop which is directly over hole 2, cut a small vertical slit in the thong with a thonging chisel or the point of a knife. Enlarge it from the rear with the fid and pass the working end through the hole in the leather and through the slit in the thong, as indicated by the arrow-line in Fig. 5.

In Fig. 6 the working end is shown through the holes in both leather and thong. Bring it down through hole 4. In that section of the loop of the thong directly over hole 3 stab another vertical slit, being careful not to cut the thong beneath. Pass the working end through hole 3 and through the slit in the thong as indicated by the arrow-line in Fig. 7. Continue for the desired length.

SPLIT-THONG APPLIQUE OF TWO THONGS—This is the same as the preceding applique except that two thongs are used and thus there is no necessity of slitting them. Work the thongs as a unit as shown in the illustrations (Figs. 9, 10, 11 and 12). One thong of one color and one of another may be used and by overlapping them each time in the rear, a pleasing, two-toned effect is achieved.

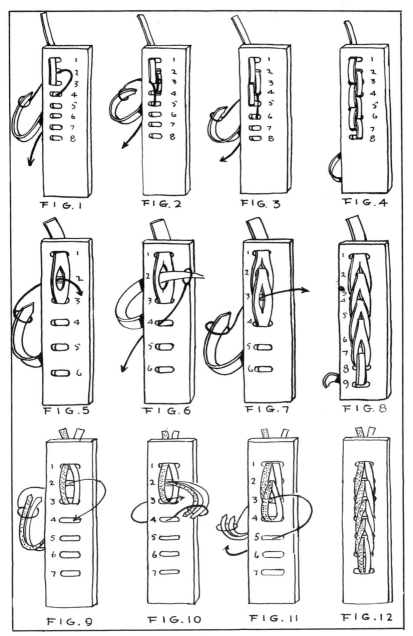

PLATE 72—Top: Chain Appliqué of One Thong.
Center: Split-Thong Appliqué.
Bottom: Split-Thong Appliqué of Two Thongs.

153

PLATE 73

HAIR BRAID APPLIQUE OF TWO THONGS—Begin this appliqué by passing two thongs of equal width through the top hole from the rear to the front (Fig. 1). The left-hand thong (unshaded) is designated as A, and the right-hand one (shaded) as B.

Pass thong A down through hole 4 and thong B down through hole 3.

The arrow-lines in Fig. 1 show the next pass of the two thongs. Bring thong B through the second hole from the top and to the extreme right of the other two thongs. Pass thong A back through the third hole from the top and to the extreme right of the other two.

In bringing both thongs from rear to front always have them emerge to the extreme right. This will incline the finished braid toward the left and if the holes are not too far from the edge of the leather or pieces of leather being joined, the braid will lie on the very edge, giving an attractive edge-lacing effect.

Pass thong B to the left over one thong, under one and down through hole 5, as indicated by the arrow-line in Fig. 2. Now pass thong A over the first thong to the left, under thong B and down through hole 6. This is indicated by the arrow-line in Fig. 3.

Bring thong B up from rear to front through hole 4 and to the right, as indicated in Fig. 4 by the arrow-line. Pass thong A up from rear to front through hole 5, as indicated by the arrow-line in Fig. 4.

In the next step, shown in Fig. 5, pass thong B over one thong (its own part) under the white thong (A) and down through hole 7. Thong A follows the corresponding path, passing over its own part, under thong B and down through hole 8, as shown in Fig. 6.

Continue this as far as desired. By tracing a design or initials on a piece of leather it can be followed with this appliquéd braid. The finished braid, shown loosely woven so the operation can better be observed, is shown in Fig. 7. The back of the braid is illustrated in Fig. 8.

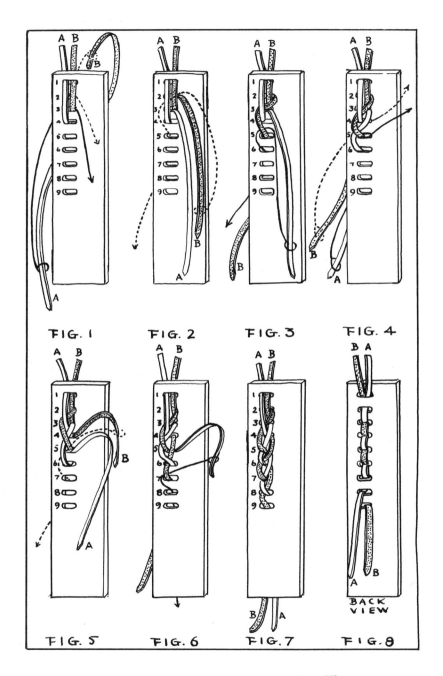

FIG. 1   FIG. 2   FIG. 3   FIG. 4

FIG. 5   FIG. 6   FIG. 7   FIG. 8

PLATE 73—Hair-Braid Appliqué of Two Thongs.

155

PLATE 74

"S" Type Applique of One Thong—The width of the thong will determine the distance of the holes from each other and the distance between the two vertical rows of holes. If a ⅛ inch thong is used and the braid is to be closed up, space the holes 3/16 of an inch from each other and the vertical rows ½ inch apart.

This appliqué, like other appliqué braids, is not only used to join two pieces of leather, but for decoration.

Pass the working end of the thong through the top hole at the right from the rear to the front and then down and across through the second hole on the left, shown in Fig. 1.

Next, bring the thong up through the top hole on the left from the rear to the front and down to the right over its own part and through hole 3 on the right-hand side. Pass it back to the front through hole 2 on the right, as indicated by the arrow-line in Fig. 2.

Incline the thong to the left over its own part and down through hole 3 on the left. Then pass it back to the front through hole 2 on the left, as indicated by the arrow-line in Fig. 3.

Incline the thong to the right, over its own part and down through hole 4 on the right-hand side. Then pass it back and up through hole 3 on the same side, as indicated by the arrow-line in Fig. 4.

Incline the thong to the left, over its own part, down through hole 4 on the left-hand side and up through hole 3 on the same side, as illustrated in Fig. 5.

Incline the thong to the right, over its own part, down through hole 5 on the right-hand side and up through hole 4 on the same side, as illustrated in Fig. 6.

Continue thus until the braid has reached the desired length. The finished braid is shown in Fig. 7, with the back view in Fig. 8. This latter figure illustrates how the ends are secured.

In Fig. 9 this appliqué is used to fasten the part of a belt that holds the buckle. The braid can be continued down the middle of the belt, the shaded portion to the left showing a *bed* or depressed part in the leather. To make this *bed,* the leather should be dampened, then cut along the sides of the bed to about one-third of its thickness and depressed with ordinary background stamping tools. The braid will then lie flat on the surface. The bed is not necessary, however, and the braid can be emphasized by working it over a narrow strip of leather laid between the rows of holes.

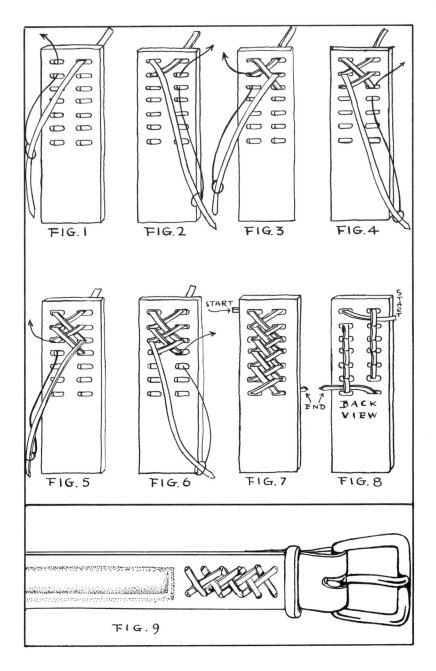

FIG. 1 FIG. 2 FIG. 3 FIG. 4

FIG. 5 FIG. 6 FIG. 7 FIG. 8

START

END BACK VIEW

START

FIG. 9

PLATE 74—"S" Type Appliqué of One Thong.

157

PLATE 75

APPLIQUE OF THREE THONGS—This beautiful appliqué of three thongs gives the effect of a five-part flat braid. The color of the thongs may be varied. It is, of course, used to fasten together parts of leather as well as for decoration. Space the rows of vertical holes about five times the width of the thong.

Thongs are designated from left to right as A, B and C. Pass thong A from the rear to front through the upper left-hand hole and down through the third right-hand hole (Fig. 1). Pass thong B through the middle upper hole from rear to front and down to the left, over thong A and through hole 3 on the left (Fig. 1); thong C through the upper right-hand hole from rear to front, under thong A and down through hole 4 on the left-hand side (Fig. 1).

Now, bring thong A (on the right) up through the second hole on the right (b) from rear to front, incline down the left, over its own part and through hole 5 on the left-hand side, as indicated by the arrow-line in Fig. 1.

Bring thong B (on the left) up through hole 2 on that side, incline down to the right and over its own part, under thong C, over thong A and down through the fourth hole (d) on the right-hand side (indicated by the arrow-line in Fig. 2). Next, bring thong C up through hole 3 on the left, incline down to the right, over its own part, under thong A and down through the fifth hole (e) as indicated by the arrow-line in Fig. 3.

Bring thong A up through hole 4 on the left, incline down to the right and over its own part and through hole "f," the sixth hole on the right (Fig. 4).

The three thongs are now on the right-hand side (Fig. 5). Pass thong B up through the third hole (c) on the right, incline down towards the left, pass it over its own part, under thong C, over thong A and down through hole 6 on the left. Bring thong C up through hole "d," the fourth one on the right, incline down toward the left, over its own part, under thong A and down through hole 7 on the left. Pass thong A up through the fifth hole on the right (e), incline down to the left, over its own part and down through the left-hand hole, 8. These moves are all indicated by arrow-lines in Fig. 5.

Fig. 6 shows the finished braid, and Fig. 7 shows the back of the braid and the method of securing the ends.

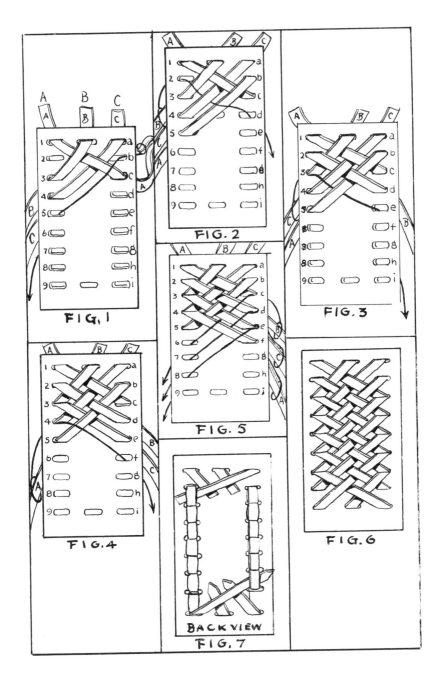

FIG. 1

FIG. 2

FIG. 3

FIG. 4

FIG. 5

FIG. 6

BACK VIEW
FIG. 7

PLATE 75—Appliqué of Three Thongs.

159

PLATE 76

APPLIQUE OF FIVE THONGS—Braiding with five thongs in the following manner gives the effect of a seven-part herringbone flat braid.

Space three holes across the top between the upper holes of the two vertical rows (Fig. 1). The thongs are designated from left to right as A, B, C, D and E. Pass thong A through the upper left-hand hole from rear to front and down through the fourth (d) right-hand hole; thong B through the second horizontal hole from the left and down to the right through the third hole (c) on the right-hand side; thong C through the third horizontal hole from the left, over thongs B and A and down through the left-hand hole, 3; thong D through the fourth horizontal hole, incline down to the left, under thong B, over thong A and down through the left-hand hole, 4; thong E through the upper right-hand hole, incline down to the left under thongs B and A and down through the fifth left-hand hole (all shown in Fig. 1).

Next, bring thong C up through hole 2 on the left, incline down to the right, over its own part, under thong D and E and down through the fifth hole (e) on the right, designated by the arrow-line in Fig. 1.

Bring thong D up through hole 3 on the left, incline down to the right, over its own part, under thong E and down through the sixth hole (f), on the right-hand side (Fig. 2). Pass thong E up through hole 4 on the left, incline down to the right, over its own part, and down through the seventh hole (g) on the right (Fig. 3).

All thongs are now on the right-hand side (Fig. 4). Start with the top one, thong B and, bring it up through the second hole on the right (b), over its own part, under two thongs, over two thongs, and down through hole 6 on the left, indicated by the arrow-line in Fig. 4.

Pass thong A up through the third hole on the right (c), down over its own part, under two thongs, over one and down through hole 7 (Fig. 5). Bring thong C up through the fourth hole on the right (d), down over its own part, under two thongs and down through hole 8 on the left (Fig. 6). Pass thong D up through the fifth hole on the right (e), down over its own part, under one and through hole 9 on the left (Fig. 7). Pass thong E up through the sixth hole on the right (f), down over its own part and through hole 10 on the left (Fig. 8).

Now work the thongs back to the right in the same manner; each goes up through the hole above, then down over its own part, under the next two and so on. The finished braid is shown in Fig. 9.

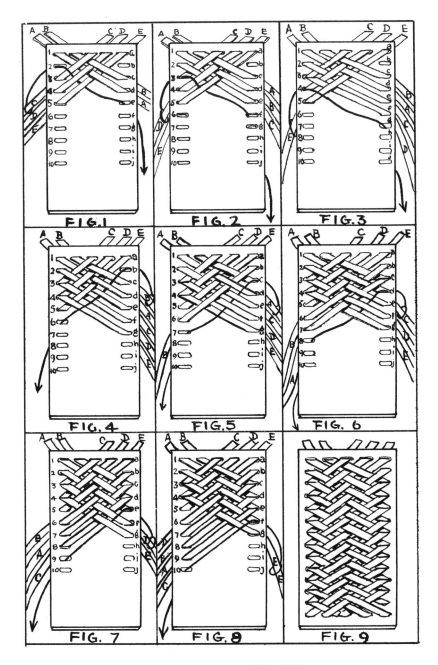

PLATE 76—Appliqué of Five Thongs.

161

PLATE 77

FIVE-THONG CIRCULAR APPLIQUE—This is the same as the five-thong appliqué in Plate 76. It gives the equivalent of a seven-part braid and when made in this circular fashion, usually is raised by placing a small strip of leather beneath, over which it is braided.

As the outer circle of holes will be spaced wider apart than those of the inner circle, be careful in laying out the circles to see that the outer holes are not too far apart and those in the inner circle too close together. There must be the same number of holes in the outer as in the inner circle.

The circles in Fig. 1 are divided into sixteen parts. Punch the holes on the inside of the outer circle and on the outer rim of the inner circle (Fig. 1). The width between the two rows of holes, the space between the holes themselves, and the width of the thongs, will all determine how close the braid is to be.

Pass thong A through hole 1 in the outer circle (all outer circle holes are numbered) from underneath and down through hole "e" in the inner circle (Fig. 2). (All inner circle holes are designated by letters). Pass thong B through hole 2 and down through hole "f;" thong C through hole 3 and down through "g;" thong D up through hole "b," over A, under B and C and down through hole 5; thong E up through hole "e," over A, and B, under C and through hole 6.

Pass thong A back through hole "d," then under its own part, and over B and C, and down through hole 7 (arrow-line in Fig. 2). Bring thong B back through "e," under its own part, over C and down through hole 8 (Fig. 3). Pass C back through "f," under its own part and down through hole 9. The working ends of all five thongs are now on the outer circle.

Start with D and pass it back through hole 4, under its own part, over E and A, under B and C, and down through hole "h." Follow the same sequence with the other thongs; pass each back through the hole to its rear, under its own part and then over and under, so that each thong from hole to hole in the finished braid will have a sequence of under one, over two, under two and over one.

To close the braid (Fig. 4), pass D under three, over one and into hole 4; C under one, over one, under one, over one and into hole 3; B under one, over three, into hole 2; A under one, over two, under two, over one and into hole "d," and E under one, over two, under two, over one into hole "c."

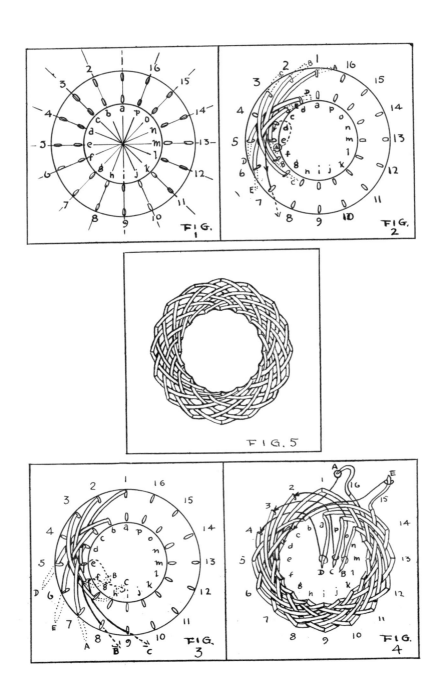

PLATE 77—Five-Thong Circular Appliqué.

163

PLATE 78

How to Make a Slit-Braid Handbag—This handbag is composed of three major parts: the top, the body and the bottom, with some thonging of varied lengths and widths. No metal attachments are necessary.

The top may be made of any soft, thin leather, such as kidskin, the kind of suede used for linings, or buckskin. Cut it to the specifications in Fig. 2, with eight equally spaced holes in the top part and thirty-one in the bottom part, as well as four on each end.

For the body of the handbag, use 6-ounce leather (Fig. 1), with thirty-one evenly spaced holes on both top and bottom. No holes on the ends are required, as the braiding thong will keep these ends together.

The bottom is a circular piece of leather of the same weight (6-ounce) as the body. Around its edge punch thirty-one evenly spaced holes. To determine the exact diameter of the bottom, divide the length of the body by 3.1416, always taking into consideration the thickness of the body piece. When the body piece is formed into a tube, the inner circumference is less than the outer circumference. As the bottom part fits into the inner circumference it would be well to cut out the bottom and then measure the body part around it before cutting it and before punching any holes.

Next, cut the body piece with vertical slits of one inch in width, beginning ½ inch from the top and stopping ½ inch from the bottom. Remember that in slit braiding of this type the slits must be of an *unequal* number. It might be well to divide the length of the body piece into nineteen equal parts, as it may have been cut a trifle longer or a trifle shorter after being measured around the bottom piece.

Weave a one-inch thong through the slits, beginning several slits to the right of the ends as shown in Fig. 6. Continue around, over one, under one, etc. Cement both ends on the inside. Now lace on the bottom as shown in Fig. 6; next, the top, and then close the ends of the top by lacing and pull through drawstrings, which may be of a small round braid.

The top should go inside the body piece, so here again, it is well to fit it before cutting. Contrasting leathers may be used in this project if desired.

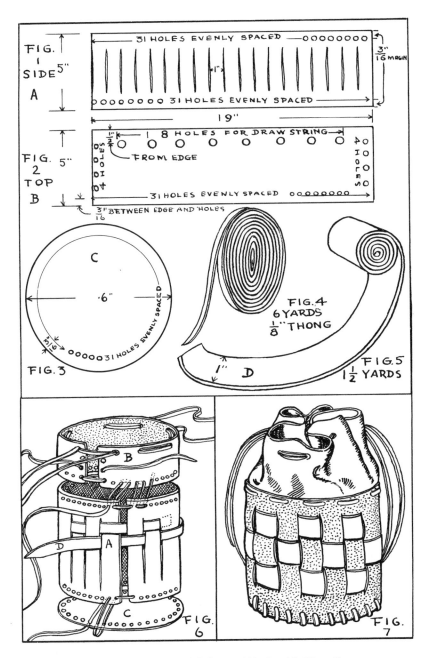

FIG. 1 SIDE A

31 HOLES EVENLY SPACED —— 00000000

5"

1"

3"/16 MARGIN

0000000 31 HOLES EVENLY SPACED ——

19"

FIG. 2 TOP B

5"

8 HOLES FOR DRAW STRING

1"

1"

10 HOLES

4 HOLES

FROM EDGE

40 HOLES

31 HOLES EVENLY SPACED 00000000

3"/16 BETWEEN EDGE AND HOLES

C

·6"

3/16 00000 31 HOLES EVENLY SPACED

FIG. 3

FIG. 4 6 YARDS 1/8" THONG

1" D

FIG. 5 1 1/2 YARDS

B

D A

C

FIG. 6

FIG. 7

PLATE 78—How to Make a Slit-Braid Handbag.

165

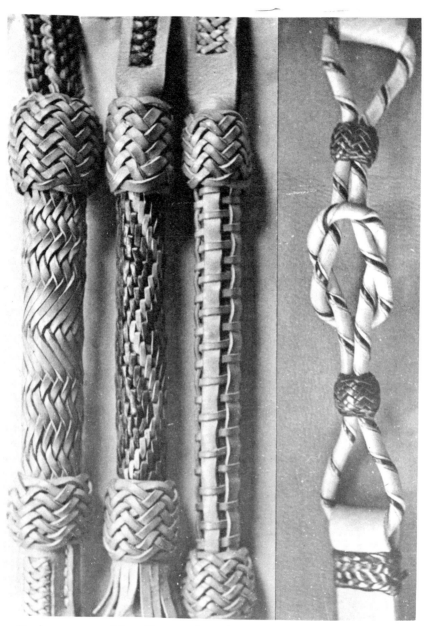

Various types of handle coverings for riding crops. Left to right: Multiple Braid Covering (Pl. 44); half-hitching zig-zag type (Pl. 41); Slit-Leather covering (Pl. 40). Pineapple-type woven knots at each end of handle-braid (Pl. 67). Use of twist braid (Pl. 13) in back part of woman's belt. This is "wormed" with black lacing. Pineapple knots (Pl. 67) and gaucho knot of three passes (Pl. 61) shown.

Top: Wrist-watch band made from Conquistador Braid (Pl. 11). Woven ring knots (Pl. 58) used as loop and coverings. Knots next to watch can be made from Headhunter's Knot (Pl. 65).

Center: Three-inch wide belt decorated in the center with applique similar to that of Plate 76 and with a four-thong round edge braid on the edges (Pl. 34).

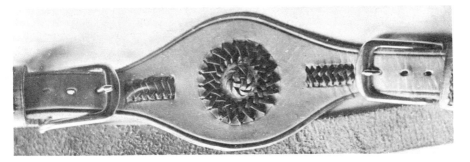

Bottom: Woman's belt (front) showing "S" type applique of one thong (Pl. 74) braided in circular fashion — also as decoration near buckles. Gaucho round button knot (Pl. 28) in center of appliqued circle.

Woman's pocketbook showing use of stairstep applique of two thongs (Pl. 71) as edge braiding as well as holding parts together.

BRAIDER'S GLOSSARY

APPLIQUE—A form of braiding which is worked directly upon the surface of the leather.

AWL—A pointed instrument or tool for piercing small holes in leather. Used when stitching with waxed thread.

BACK—The middle of the hide or skin directly over the backbone. This section supplies the best thongs.

BACK BRAID—A braid in which the thongs are first braided loosely in an over-one-under-one sequence, then crowned and woven back upon themselves.

BRAID—The interlacing or weaving of one thong with itself or several thongs with each other.

BASKET-WEAVE—Usually where the interwoven thongs are of an over-one-under-one sequence.

BLANKET-STITCH—A form of lock stitch. Sometimes called buttonhole stitch in edge-braiding.

BASIL—A cheap form of sheepskin.

BELLY—The sides of a skin or hide. A very thin thong can be cut from this section. However, it must be dampened and stretched before the thong is cut.

BEVEL—To cut or shape to a bevel angle; to slope the edge or surface of a piece of leather.

BIGHT—A loop in a thong, as that part of the thong between the working end and standing end, formed by bringing the working end of the thong around, near to, or across its own part. Particularly, the "scallops" on the upper and lower edges of a turk's head or woven knot.

BUCKSKIN—A soft, pliable leather of deer skin, formerly tanned by the American Indians by treating them with brains of the animals and smoking the skins. Today a chrome process is used and the term applies to both deer and elk skins.

BUTTON—Interwoven thongs forming a knot, or a strip of leather rolled into a small cylinder.

CATGUT—A tough cord obtained from the intestines of sheep. Used for violin strings, tennis rackets, surgical sutures, and for turk's-head decorations on canes and whips. Also for ferrules on the latter.

CALFSKIN—Leather made from the skins of calves. The best and most attractive thongs are cut from calfskin.

CHAMOIS—A very soft leather made from sheepskin.

COACHWHIPPING—A braid made around a core in which several thongs are worked as one unit.

CORE—A hard or pliable center of a whip, quirt or crop, usually of twisted rawhide or leather, but sometimes of rattan or French willow. Also a rope center of a braid.

CROWN KNOT—A knot at the end of a braid where the working ends are laid over each other so that they interlock and are pointing back toward the braid.

DRAW GAUGE—A hand tool for cutting thongs or leather straps.

EDGE LACING—A type of edge braiding in which the braid covers the edge of the leather. While a decoration it also serves to fasten two or more pieces of leather together.

FALSE BRAID—Braid where leather thongs are pulled alternately through slits in their own parts. Usually termed slit braiding and simulates actual braiding.

FID—Sometimes called belt awl in leather work. A long tapering metal tool with a blunt point used for making an opening between thongs in braiding, as well as enlarging slits through which thongs are passed.

FLAT BRAID—Braid in which thongs are worked alternately from each side.

FLESH SIDE—The inner or rough side of the leather as opposed to the smooth or hair side.

GRAIN—The smooth natural exterior surface of leather from which the hair has been removed. Same as hair side or smooth side.

GUILLOCHE—A pattern made by interlacing curved lines in which braiding is simulated, sometimes carved or stamped on leather.

HAIR BRAID—The simple, three-thong flat braid.

HERRINGBONE—A pattern usually of a V-shape formed by thongs when braided in over-two-under-two sequence or over-three-under-three sequence.

HIDE—A pelt from one of the larger animals. Cattlehide, cowhide, horsehide, etc.

HIDE ROPE—Rope made from strips of leather cut from green hides and braided. Formerly used by seamen in rigging.

HONDA—The eye in a lariat through which a braided leather rope or *reata* is rove.

HUARACHES—Mexican sandal-like shoes with tops of braided thongs.

INCISING—Another name for leather carving. A method of cutting around the ornament slightly with a knife before sinking the background.

INLAY—A combination of two leathers where the braidwork is set in the other, the two surfaces near level.

INTERLACED—Where laces or thongs cross alternately over and under each other.

KINK—Twist in a thong.

LACE—A small, narrow thong. Usually commercially made and beveled; used mainly for edge-braiding or edge-lacing.

LACING NEEDLE—Flat needle split at one end to receive the thong or lacing.

LATIGO—A form of thong of alum-tanned leather; often mistermed rawhide.

LOCK—Thonging in which each turn secures itself.

LIE—The "settling down" of a thong in the right position, usually obtained by tapping it lightly with a mallet.

MANDREL—A cylindrical or conical core used in making turk's heads or woven knots.

MARLINSPIKE—A metal pin tapering to a point used in separating thongs in braiding. Synonymous with fid.

NATURAL—A term applied to unstained or undyed leather.

PARFLECHE—Rawhide.

PARING—Thinning down the edge of the leather with a knife.

PILE—The under or flesh side of leather. Also called the velvet side.

PINKING—Cutting the border of leather in an ornamental pattern of small scallops with indented edges.

PLAIT (PLAT)—The continued interlacing of several thongs to form a braided strap. In some sections plait means a round braid and "braid" is used for flat braid.

PRONG—Tool for punching several slots at equal spacings.

PULLING—A skin is more elastic from side to side than from neck to tail.

PUNCH—A tool with a sharpened cylinder or tube which acts upon a soft metal base for punching holes in leather. There are also independent punches known as drive punches. The revolving punch has as many as six different size tubes.

RAWHIDE—An untanned hide.

ROUND BRAID—A braid in which alternate thongs are brought around to the rear instead of straight across as in flat braiding.

RUN—The passage of a thong from one hole to another on the front of the leather, without going over the edge to the back.

SADDLE LEATHER—A vegetable tanned cowhide leather, tan or natural colored.

SADDLE SOAP—A special soap used to cleanse and soften leather.

SADDLE-STAMP—A metal stamp to impress various designs on leather.

SKIN—The pelt of the smaller animals, such as calf, goat, sheep, etc.

SKIVING—Splitting a skin horizontally into several thicknesses. Beveling an edge by paring.

SLOT—A long, narrow aperture as distinct from a round punched hole.

SPANISH KNOT—A woven cylindrical knot of one thong worked with a turk's head as a skeleton or base.

SPANISH LACING—Edge-braiding or edge-lacing.

SQUARE BRAID—Braid usually made by the overlapping or crowning of several thongs.

STANDING END—The inactive or secured part of a thong as opposed to the active or working part.

THONG—A narrow strip cut from a hide or skin. Sometimes beveled on the flesh side.

THONGING CHISEL—A small chisel with one or more tines or prongs to cut slits for thonging.

THONG WHEEL—A tool cutting a continuous line of slots for thonging when rolled under pressure.

TRICK BRAID—An inside braid made with three or more thongs cut in a strap in such a manner that the ends are joined.

TUBE PUNCH—Same as revolving punch.

TURK'S HEAD—A braided wreath or ring in which the braid is similar to that of flat braids but is continuous and made with one thong. A turk's head cannot have the same number of thongs across its breadth as bights. The law is that bights and parts must not have a common divisor or the working end will come back to the standing end before the knot is complete.

TWIST BRAID—Braid made with leather turned or twisted upon itself

WORKING END—The end of a thong used in making a braid as distinguished from standing end.

More Hobby and How-To Books . . .

ENCYCLOPEDIA OF KNOTS AND FANCY ROPEWORK
Raoul Graumont & John Hensel
Complete coverage of the subject of tying knots and making ornamental rope designs as well as a history of knots and rope making. Profusely illustrated.

BRAIDING RAWHIDE HORSE TACK
Robert L. Woolery
Here is an instruction manual for the novice worker in rawhide. Assuming no previous knowledge or experience on the part of the reader, the author starts with the fresh cowhide, continues through cutting and braiding, and ends with finished reatas, bosals, hobbles, and reins.

HOW TO MAKE COWBOY HORSE GEAR AND HOW TO MAKE A WESTERN SADDLE
Bruce Grant & Lee M. Rice
An illustrated volume showing from beginning to end how to make articles used daily by horsemen for work and show. Photographs depict the finished articles and reveal their evolution from the old worlds of Mexico and South America to the United States.

WHIPS AND WHIPMAKING
David W. Morgan
A comprehensive introduction to whips, telling what whips were used for various jobs, why they are designed as they are, how they are made, and how they are used.

For full information about these and other Cornell Maritime Press and Tidewater Publishers titles, inquire at your bookstore, craft shop or:

Cornell Maritime Press, Inc.
Centreville, Maryland 21617